Great Ancient EGYPT Projects

You Can Build Yourself

Carmella Van Vleet

Image Credits

pg. 26, ruins: from wikipedia commons, photo by Hajor, December 2001; pg. 43, Senet: from wikipedia, courtesy of The Yorck Project; pg. 73, Pharaoh Akhenaton: from wikipedia commons; pg. 84, Lighthouse of Alexandria: computer visualization by Bill Munns; pg. 96, mummy: courtesy of House of Pharaoh (www.house-of-pharaoh.com), artwork by Kameron Rieck, photo by Gabriele Zoulek; pg. 102, King Tut: courtesy of Egypt's Supreme Council of Antiquities; pg. 110, Jean-François Champollion: from wikipedia; pg. 111, Rosetta stone, from wikipedia, photo courtesy of Matija Podhraški; images courtesy of Dover Publications: iii, vi, 5, 8, 10–12, 15, 17, 26–30, 35, 36, 40, 41, 47, 48, 51, 54, 55, 61–63, 72, 73, 80, 82, 86, 89, 91, 92, 94, 97, 98, 100–102, 104, 106, 109, 112–118, 121, 122.

Nomad Press
A division of Nomad Communications
10 9 8 7 6 5 4 3

Printed in the United States.
ISBN: 978-0-97712-945-4
Questions regarding the ordering of this book should be addressed to
Independent Publishers Group
814 N. Franklin St.
Chicago, IL 60610
www.ipgbook.com

Nomad Press
2456 Christian St.
White River Junction, VT 05001
www.nomadpress.net

Table of Contents

Timeline of Ancient Egypt's History

Most experts like to break up ancient Egypt's history into the following time periods:

Early Dynastic Period, c. 3100–2686 BCE

- Menes, the first Egyptian pharaoh, unites Upper and Lower Egypt. He establishes the capital at what was later known as Memphis.
- Hieroglyphic script is developed.

Old Kingdom, c. 2686–2181 BCE

- The pharaohs are like god-kings and become very powerful, building many pyramids.
- Irrigation of the Nile River allows the Egyptians to grow more food and Egypt's population increases.
- King Khufu builds the Great Pyramid of Giza and the Great Sphinx.

First Intermediate Period, c. 2181–2055 BCE

- The pharaohs lose power and Egypt splits apart and enters a chaotic time.
- No pyramids are built.

Middle Kingdom, c. 2055–1650 BCE

- The pharaohs become powerful again and reunite Egypt.
- The Egyptians take control of Nubia, which has valuable resources like gold and semi-precious stones.
- The last pyramids are built.

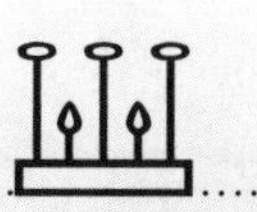

Second Intermediate Period, c. 1650–1550 BCE

- Asian invaders take over northeastern Egypt.

New Kingdom, c. 1550–1069 BCE

- The pharaohs reunite Egypt again and queens are more powerful than before. Some queens become pharaohs.
- Trade with Asia grows.
- Many great temples are built.
- The most famous pharaoh, King Tutankhamen, rules from 1336 to 1327 BCE.

Third Intermediate Period, c. 1069–644 BCE

- Egypt falls apart and the Nubians in the south regain their independence.
- Many cities are developed.
- Foreigners invade and take over Egypt, first the Nubians in 728 BCE, then the Assyrians, from Mesopotamia (now modern Iraq), in 669 BCE.

Late Period, c. 644–332 BCE

- The Persians, from the Near East (now Syria, Jordan, Lebanon, and Israel), conquer Egypt in 525 BCE.
- Demotic script is developed.

Greek & Roman Egypt, c. 322 BCE–639 CE

- Alexander the Great, from Macedonia (north of Greece), conquers Egypt with a Greek army in 332 BCE.
- The Greeks rule Egypt starting in 323 BCE, bringing Greek culture and language to Egypt.
- The Rosetta stone is carved in 196 BCE.
- Cleopatra, the last Greek pharaoh, dies in 30 BCE.
- Augustus, the emperor of the Roman Empire, conquers Egypt. The Romans rule Egypt for more than 600 years.

BCE stands for Before the Common Era and means the same as BC (which stands for Before Christ).
CE stands for Common Era and means the same as AD (or *anno Domini*).

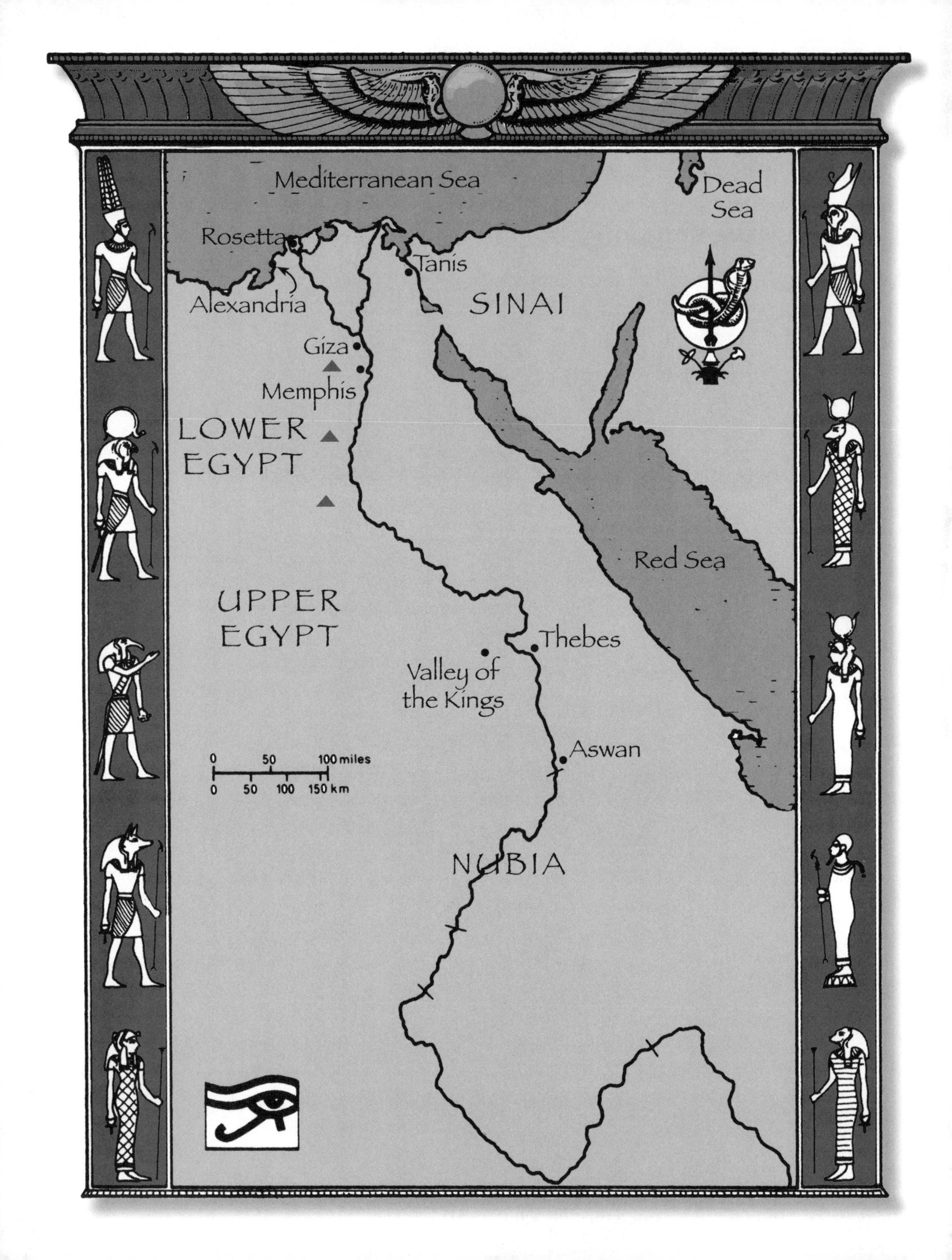
Mediterranean Sea
Dead Sea
Rosetta
Tanis
Alexandria
SINAI
Giza
Memphis
LOWER EGYPT
Red Sea
UPPER EGYPT
Thebes
Valley of the Kings
Aswan
0 50 100 miles
0 50 100 150 km
NUBIA

Introduction

Have you ever looked at a picture of a **pyramid**, a mummy, or an ancient clay pot with **hieroglyphs** and wondered who made it? Or have you ever been to a museum and seen a statue of a **pharaoh** or an Egyptian peasant and been curious about who these people were and what their lives were like thousands of years ago?

Ancient Egypt existed from about 3100 BCE to about 639 CE, and it was one of the most powerful civilizations of all time. For reasons that we will explore in this book, ancient Egyptian people, thought, and culture have always fascinated the modern world. What was it about these things that made this civilization so strong?

Words to Know

pyramid: monuments that house the tombs of ancient Egyptian pharaohs, as well as all the things he needed in the afterlife. There were three types of pyramids built in ancient Egypt: step pyramids, bent pyramids, and true pyramids.

hieroglyphs: the pictures and symbols that made up ancient Egypt's earliest form of writing. Hieroglyphs means "sacred writing," and often covered coffins and the walls of tombs and temples.

pharaoh: the ancient Egyptian name for a king.

Centuries and centuries after the last pharaoh died, tourists continue to travel by the thousands to the ancient pyramids, and all over the world people line up for hours at museums and galleries to view exhibits of ancient Egyptian art, architecture, and other relics that shed light on ancient Egyptian life and times.

Because Egypt's dry desert sands naturally preserved many tombs, temples, and artifacts, we know a good deal about ancient Egypt and its people. It would be nearly impossible for one book to cover everything about this civilization, but this book will help you understand what life was like for its people. It explores what ancient Egyptians ate and wore, where they lived and what tools they used, and it also investigates the often mysterious subjects of pharaohs, pyramids, mummies, and tombs.

Most of the projects in this book can be made with little adult supervision and materials that you already have at your house. So step back into an ancient time, and get ready to **Build It Yourself**.

1 The Foundations of Ancient Egypt

The Greek writer Herodotus once described Egypt as the "gift of the Nile," and it's easy to understand why. The annual flooding of the **Nile River** provided ancient Egyptians with rich soil that was ideal for farming in the middle of a great desert. The Nile also provided a way of traveling and of trading goods, while acting as a natural barrier against ancient Egypt's enemies. In many ways, the Nile made life possible in ancient Egypt. And what a life it was!

Modern-day Egypt is at the northeastern part of Africa. The Mediterranean Sea and the Red Sea border it to the north and east; the countries of Libya and Sudan border it to the west and south. Ancient Egypt covered roughly the same territory, but it extended farther south into Sudan. Egypt lies within the Sahara Desert, the largest and hottest desert in the world. (The whole continental United

Why Is Egypt Upside Down?

Ancient Egypt was divided into two areas: **Upper Egypt** and **Lower Egypt**. If you look at a map of ancient Egypt, you'll see something strange: Upper Egypt is *below* Lower Egypt! The reason for this "upside-down" characteristic is that the Nile, unlike most rivers, flows south to north. Therefore, Lower Egypt is actually near the top of the continent, near the Nile's delta. A delta is the triangular-shaped area where a river fans out and divides as it flows into a larger body of water. These two distinct areas of ancient Egypt are often called the Two Lands. When these two lands were unified under one ruler, the ancient capital was Memphis, which was near their border. Without concrete evidence, Egyptologists can only guess as to when Upper and Lower Egypt united. Many believe a king named Menes brought them under one rule around 3100 BCE.

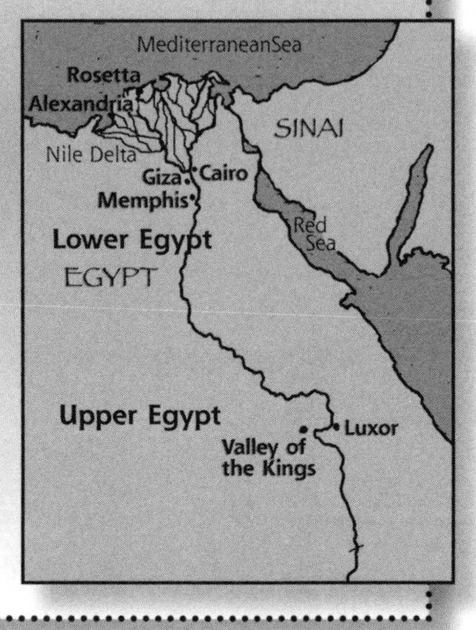

States would fit inside the Sahara!) Deserts receive little rainfall, so Egypt's climate is hot and dry, especially in the southern part of the country, nearest the equator. During the day, the temperature can easily exceed 100 degrees Fahrenheit, and it has been recorded as high as 136 degrees. At night, the temperature may fall to about 50 degrees. There are hot winds in the spring called **khamsin**, which raise air temperatures even higher than those of the summer and cause terrible sandstorms.

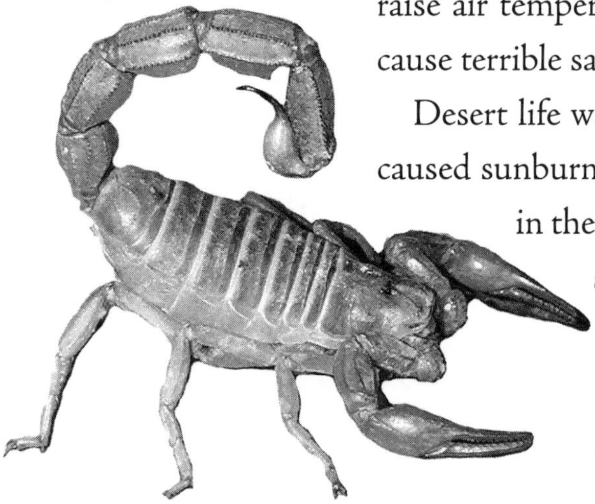

A scorpion.

Desert life was hard for the ancient Egyptians. The blazing sun caused sunburn and dehydration. There were poisonous creatures in the desert, such as scorpions, as well as the harsh sandstorms. Even when there weren't sandstorms, sand found its way into everything, including food, which wore down many ancient Egyptians' teeth. As harsh as the Egyptian climate is, it helped preserve many artifacts from ancient times. Pottery, art, tombs, temples, and even bodies are still around for us to study thanks to the desert sands and dry weather.

Harvesting.

While some ancient Egyptians lived in the heart of the desert, most of them lived along the banks of the Nile. This is where the land was fertile for farming, and, of course, where it was easiest to get water.

Ancient Egypt was largely an agricultural civilization. People depended on the annual flooding of the Nile, which was caused mainly by the monsoon rains in central Africa. This flooding was called the **inundation** and lasted for several months each year. It left behind rich soil perfect for farming. Ancient Egyptians farmers lived simple lives but kept a variety of animals and grew a variety of crops, ranging from wheat to vegetables to fruits. Harvesting was a big job. At harvest time, everyone, including the children, pitched in. Animals sometimes pulled plows, and there were simple machines to help draw water from the Nile, but most of the work was done by hand.

On the whole, Egyptians were excellent farmers, but they were experts at other things, too. Ancient Egypt was home to some of the world's most skilled artisans and builders. Glass beads, jewelry, pottery, and other pieces of art from Egypt were highly prized throughout the ancient world. The temples and pyramids that the ancient Egyptians built to honor their many gods and to entomb their dead pharaohs were big

A falcon necklace.

The Great Pyramids at Giza.

attractions thousands of years ago just as they are today. People traveled from around the ancient world to see them.

Pyramids are gigantic stone tombs constructed for ancient Egyptian royalty. They have square bases and triangular walls that meet in a point at the top. It took hundreds of years of trial and error to learn how to construct a true pyramid. A few interesting and unsuccessful attempts, such as the Bent Pyramid, are still around for us to see. Eventually, ancient Egyptians became experts in the design and building of these intriguing structures. The Great Pyramid of Giza was so well designed, for example, that there's no room for even a piece of paper between the stones!

In addition to their pyramids, ancient Egyptians are famous for their mummies. They preserved bodies through **mummification** because they believed the body was needed in the afterlife. Sometimes scary looking, but always fascinating, mummies have taught us much about ancient Egyptian religious beliefs.

Family was very important to ancient Egyptians. Children were loved and valued, and

The Bent Pyramid of King Snefru in Dashur.

women enjoyed many of the same rights as men. For example, women could own businesses—and there were even women pharaohs! However, throughout most of ancient Egypt's history, evidence suggests that under normal circumstances women were of a lower social status than men. There are no records, for instance, of women being educated as scribes. And other than the wives and daughters of royalty, women were rarely given government positions.

Ancient Egyptians worked hard, but they also enjoyed music, dance, food, and art. Children had pets and toys and played tug-a-war, leap frog, and board games such as Senet. (Even kings and queens loved to play Senet!) It wasn't all fun and games for ancient Egyptian children, however; they had chores, lessons, and worship. In this respect, ancient Egyptian children weren't all that different from you!

Ancient Egypt thrived for over 3,000 years and fell from power over 2,000 years ago. How do we know so much about such an old civilization? First

Words to Know

Nile River: the longest river in the world and the reason the ancient Egyptians survived and thrived so well.

khamsin: hot winds that raise the air temperature and cause terrible sandstorms during Egypt's spring.

inundation: the annual flooding of the Nile during ancient times.

mummification: the process of drying and preserving a body.

Pyramid of Power

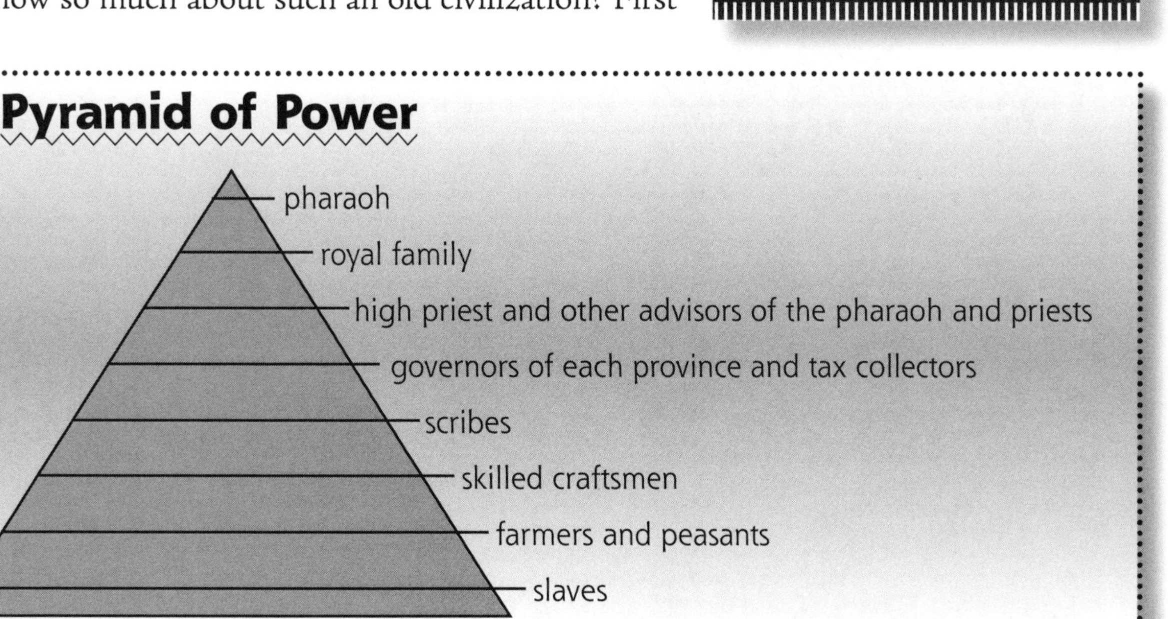

of all, **archaeologists** (who study past cultures by recovering and studying artifacts) have dug up and studied everyday objects from ancient Egypt. An Egyptologist is an archaeologist or scholar who specializes in Egyptology, or the study of ancient Egypt. Secondly, we learned a great deal by studying ancient Egyptian buildings, such as temples and pyramids. The artifacts left behind in these buildings—furniture, jewelry, and models of boats—as well as the artwork painted on the walls, demonstrates what life was like in ancient Egypt. Texts (writing on papyrus, wall paintings, and inscriptions) from ancient Egypt also clue us in to ancient Egyptian life and beliefs. The Greek writer, Herodotus, recorded many stories and details about life in ancient Egypt. (Some experts suspect Herodotus didn't really visit Egypt but wrote down the stories he heard from travelers.) And the Bible also provides details about ancient Egypt.

Fishing on the Nile.

But for all our digging, studying, and reading, we still don't know everything about ancient Egypt. One obstacle in learning about ancient Egypt is that ancient Egyptians kept records differently than we do and removed parts of history they didn't like. For instance, if ancient Egyptians didn't like a ruler, they removed his or her name from works of art, buildings, and texts. So there is a lot we may never know!

Words to Know

archaeologist: someone who studies ancient people and their cultures.

Egyptologist: an archaeologist who specializes in Egyptology, or the study of ancient Egypt.

Upper Egypt: the land in the Nile River Valley in the southern part of ancient Egypt.

Lower Egypt: the land near the Nile's delta, in the northern part of ancient Egypt.

2 Boats

The Nile is the world's longest river, and it provided ancient Egyptians with most of what they needed to create a flourishing society—food and water, a means of travel for trading and transporting materials, and natural protection from their enemies. Because the Nile was so central to their lives, ancient Egyptians became excellent boat builders.

Since the trees native to Egypt, such as acacia and sycamore, didn't produce long enough planks or strong enough wood for boat building, the ancient Egyptians used **papyrus**, a tall marsh plant with strong stems. The ancient Egyptians used the stems, or reeds, to make boats.

To make papyrus boats, Egyptians bundled papyrus reeds together with rope. Rope was made by twisting fibers from the papyrus plant together. Boat builders used as many reeds as possible, because the wider the bundle, the more stable the boat. Each bundle contained hundreds of reeds. Some were so big around that an adult man could barely wrap his arms around it. A small, one-person boat might be made of just a few bundles, while boats intended to hold several people might be built of six or more bundles.

Papyrus plant.

Lashing bundles together to make a papyrus boat.

The Nile River

The Nile River is the longest river in the world. It is about 4,200 miles long and runs from eastern Africa to the Mediterranean, through nine countries: Uganda, Sudan, Egypt, Ethiopia, Zaire, Kenya, Tanzania, Rwanda, and Burundi. It has two main source rivers: the Blue Nile and the White Nile. Over thousands of years, the Nile has changed course. (All rivers change over time: weather, changes to the face of the land, and other forces, such as dams put up by humans, affect them.) In ancient Egypt, the Nile fanned out into lots of branches just past Memphis. This area, which was like a triangle, was known as the delta because it resembled the Greek letter *delta*.

During inundation, which is when the Nile floods, the Nile moves at about 4 knots. During the dry season it moves much slower, around 1 knot. Because of this, a boat trip that took 1 week during inundation would take 4 weeks during the dry season.

Papyrus boats had a distinct look: the ends of them curved slightly upward, making a crescent shape. Boatmen steered with long poles or oars. Bigger boats required more manpower to move, while one or two people could power the smaller boats along. Because the necessary materials were plentiful and easy to find, papyrus boats became the most popular type of boat in ancient Egypt, especially among peasants who couldn't afford fancier boats made of wood from far off lands. Papyrus boats like the ones the ancient Egyptians built are still used in parts of the world today.

Papyrus boats were just fine for hunting, fishing, and traveling short distances, but they weren't very useful if you wanted to go long distances or had to transport large, heavy loads, like the heavy blocks that were used to build pyramids! For these tasks, Egyptians invented wooden boats with sails. There's evidence that dates back

Papyrus boat.

Did You Know?

Hapy (also spelled Hapi) was the god of the Nile. His name means "running one," probably referring to the Nile's current. The annual flooding of the Nile was sometimes said to be the arrival of Hapy.

Hapy

to the Old Kingdom (2686–2181 BCE) that Egyptians were the first to make planked boats. In 1991, archaeologists discovered 14 boats buried near Abydos, an ancient town in Upper Egypt. These boats, each 75 feet long, are known as the Abydos ships and are thought to be the world's oldest planked boats.

Though the local wood was not ideal for boat building, ancient Egyptians came up with ways of constructing wooden boats from small native trees by using planks that were only about 3 feet long. Some boats were made of cedar wood imported from what is now the country of Lebanon. The ancient Egyptians didn't have nails, so the planks were joined with wooden pegs or "sewn" together by weaving rope in and out of the bundles.

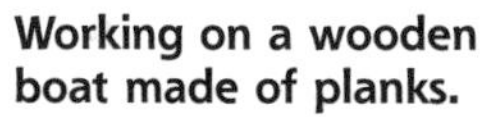
Working on a wooden boat made of planks.

Ra's Journey

Ra (sometimes spelled Re or Rah) was the ancient Egyptian sun god. According to the ancient Egyptians, Ra was the creator of the world, and the rising and setting of the sun each day was the symbol of his creation. Each night, Ra journeyed across the "ocean" sky into the afterlife. One of the earliest drawings of this journey showed Ra aboard a papyrus boat. For this reason, papyrus boats had religious significance. Because the Egyptians believed that the spirit of a person who died traveled with Ra into the afterlife, a boat or a model of a boat was put into every tomb.

Ancient Egyptians made sails out of woven linen or reeds. The wind typically blows against the current of the Nile, making it easy to travel south. Traveling north was also easy, because all you had to do was let the current carry you! Even when the wind didn't cooperate, ancient Egyptians could row with wooden oars.

Words to Know

papyrus: a tall, marsh plant the ancient Egyptians used to make boats and paper. Also the actual paper made from the plant.

Hapy: the Egyptian god of the Nile and inundation.

Ra: the ancient Egyptian sun god.

As time went on, sails grew in size, rudders were added, and Egyptian boats got bigger, more durable, and easier to maneuver. Some wealthy families traveled on the Nile in boats that were over 30 feet long with cabins and a dozen oarsmen; other wealthy families may even have owned large fleets of boats so that they could take their servants when they traveled! Large boats were also often used to transport pyramid stones from the quarries.

Wooden boats constructed in the shape of fancy papyrus boats are called papyriform boats. These vessels were used by royalty for pleasure or as part of religious events like moving a statue of a god. They were also used as funeral boats, carrying pharaohs to their final resting places. One of the best-known examples of a papyriform boat is the Royal Ship of Khufu. Discovered in 1954, the 1,200 dismantled pieces of this ship were carefully put back together, like a giant puzzle. The 150-foot-long ship is in a special museum built on the spot it was found, near the Great Pyramid of Giza, just outside of Cairo (which is Egypt's current capital).

Did You Know?

Those who traveled the Nile had many dangerous animals to deal with. These included hippos, crocodiles, venomous snakes, and land animals such as lions and hyenas that came to the river to drink and hunt.

Build Your Own

Papyrus Boat

1 Pinch one end of a straw and insert it into another straw to create one big straw. Make sure the bendable parts of the straws are on the outside ends. Set it aside and do the same thing with the remaining straws. You should have 10 long straws when you're finished.

2 Use a piece of duct tape around the middle to secure all the straws together. This will give your boat more stability and keep the straws from breaking apart. A good way to do this is to lay a piece of long tape on a table, sticky side up, then carefully lay the straws down and fold the tape over them. Then gently bend the straws so they curve up like a "U."

tie straws together with string or yarn

duct tape

view of the end of the straws showing "U" formation

3 Bend the ends of the straws into a 45- to 90-degree angle. Pinch them together and tie them with a piece of string. The string should be halfway between the bend and the top of the straws. Make sure the string knot is as tight as you can get it so it doesn't slide off. Do the same thing on the other side. Snip off any extra string, and cut the tops of the straws so they are all about the same height.

4 Add a piece of tape around each end where the straws bend. You can also weave string in and out of the straws to keep them close to each other. Remember, the ancient Egyptians used ropes to sew bundles of reeds together. It's okay if the tape doesn't cover all the bendy parts.

5 If you want to, you can put a long piece of tape along the bottom of your boat to help seal it. Your boat will still float without tape on the bottom, though it might leak a little.

6 Follow the directions on the spray paint can to paint your boat and make it look more like a real reed boat. Make sure the paint is completely dry before touching it. Now, you're ready to put your boat in water and watch it float!

Variation: You can also use straw or pieces of thick, dry grass if you have some. Simply gather the pieces of straw or grass together, tie the ends with string, and then use your hands to shape a boat. You won't need tape or paint.

Time Needed

15 minutes

not including drying time

3 Farming

Imagine a place where flooding is actually a good thing. That's how it was in ancient Egypt! Every year the Nile flooded in a process called inundation. The floods left behind a rich, black soil full of minerals from the riverbed. This soil made it easier for ancient Egyptians to grow crops in the Nile Valley.

Life in ancient Egypt was divided into three seasons: ***Akhet***, ***Peret***, and ***Shemu***. *Akhet* (June to September) was the flooding season.

During *Akhet*, the river rose and covered farmlands completely. Since no farming could be done, many farmers worked for the pharaoh during this season, helping to build temples and pyramids or other public buildings.

Peret (October to February) was the growing season (also called the season of emergence). Life was busy and challenging during these months—there was much to be done. Plowing the fields and planting seeds was hard work.

Plowing and planting.

Work had to be done by hand, although sometimes animals (oxen or pigs) were used to plow or to plod down the soil over the seeds. Still, the animals had to be directed and controlled, and this meant the farmer had to walk alongside them in the hot sun.

Shemu (March to May) was the harvesting season. This season was just as busy and demanding as *Peret*. Everyone was called on to help. The men used sickles to cut down stalks of grain. Women and children gathered the stalks and **winnowed** the grain by tossing the stalks in the air so that the wind carried away everything but the seeds, which were heavier and fell to the ground.

Winnowing grain.

Harvesting lasted from sunup to sundown. Farmers worked hard to gather as much of their crop as they could. Successful harvests were important—not only for food, but for paying taxes. Before the harvest, a government surveyor would visit each farmer's fields and predict how much crop his land would produce. The amount of taxes a farmer had to pay was based on this estimate, and this amount didn't change—even if his crop was ruined by drought or eaten by roaming animals!

Harvesting figs.

Ancient Egyptian farmers grew many different kinds of crops. These included barley (used to make beer), emmer wheat (used to make bread), vegetables (such as onions, garlic, beans, chickpeas, lettuce, radishes, cabbage, and cucumbers), and fruit (such as figs, dates, grapes, and pomegranates). They also grew flowers and all kinds of spices (such as cinnamon, cumin, dill, mustard, and thyme).

Did You Know?

Ancient Egyptians recorded dates according to their Pharaoh's reign, the season, and the day. For example, "Year 3 of the reign of Rameses II, 2nd month of Akhet, day 10."

The Egyptian Calendar

Because the flooding, or inundation, of the Nile was so important to their way of life, ancient Egyptians needed a way to keep track of exactly when it would be coming. They created a calendar based on the annual appearance of Sirius, a star in the Canis Major constellation in the night sky. (Canis Major is one of Orion's hunting dogs.) Creators of the calendar chose Sirius because it showed up around the time of inundation.

The Egyptian calendar was similar to our calendar. It had 12 months, and each month had 30 days. At the end of the year, there were 5 extra days. This made a total of 365 days. The problem with this, of course, is that a solar year is just a bit longer than 365 days. We adjust for this by adding a day every 4 years, called leap year. The ancient Egyptians didn't make this adjustment, and so their calendar quickly fell out of sync. In other words, their calendar might say it was time for the inundation when it was really time to plant!

Eventually, in 238 BCE, King Ptolemy III introduced Egypt to the Julian calendar. This system, developed under Julius Caesar's rule of the ancient Roman empire, did use leap years. The Julian calendar worked better than the Egyptian calendar, although it still wasn't completely accurate. The Gregorian calendar we use today was introduced in 1582 CE.

Flax.

One very important crop was flax. **Flax** seed was made into highly prized oil. Flax fibers were used to make **linen** cloth, string, and rope. Linen cloth, along with grain and papyrus, was often exported to neighboring countries. Farmers also raised livestock like cattle, sheep, and goats for their skin, milk, and meat.

The tools farmers used to plant and harvest their fields were simple. Hoes and plows were made with wood. Early sickles were made with wood and stone "teeth." Water was critical to healthy crops, and since Egypt had such a dry climate, farmers invented ways to **irrigate** their crops using canals and basins. Canals were long ditches through which water traveled to a basin, or shallow pool,

Did You Know?

The Nile no longer floods each year; modern dams prevent it.

Did You Know?

Egyptians called their land *Kemet* (or "Black Land") because of the rich earth left behind after the flooding. The surrounding area, desert that was mostly a reddish-yellow color, was called *Deshret* (or "Red Land").

in the field. Farmers used buckets to scoop up water and poured it over the crops. But how did the farmers get the water into the canals in the first place? They used a tool called a **shaduf**.

A shaduf is a simple device that is still used in Egypt and other parts of the world today. It is made up of a bucket and a counterweight, and it draws water from a river, stream, or lake. A counterweight on one end of a pole helps to lift heavy containers full of water that can then be emptied into a canal. In ancient times, the container was made with animal skin or reeds woven tightly together.

A farmer using a shaduf to irrigate his fields.

Words to Know

Akhet: what the ancient Egyptians called the flooding season, from June to September.

Peret: what the ancient Egyptians called their growing season, from October to February. It was also called the Season of Emergence.

Shemu: what the ancient Egyptians called their harvesting season, from March to May.

winnow: to separate grain from its husks by tossing it in the air or blowing air through it.

flax: a plant whose seed was used to make oil and whose fibers were made into linen cloth.

linen: fabric woven with fibers from the flax plant.

irrigate: to supply water by diverting streams or digging canals.

shaduf: an irrigation device that the ancient Egyptians used to water their crops.

Make Your Own

Shaduf

1 Lean the tops of the four shorter branches together. The tops should crisscross, like the top of a Native American teepee. You might need a friend to help hold up the branches.

2 Use some of the rope to secure the branch tops together. Be sure to tie a knot at the end. When you're done, the branches should be able to stand up without anyone supporting them. This is the base for your shaduf.

3 Lay a long branch on the ground. (This will be the pole.) Attach the bricks to one end of the pole with the bandage or duct tape. Then attach some rope to the other end of the pole.

4 Tie the S hook at the end of the dangling rope, then hang the handle of the bucket from this hook.

5 Lay the pole into the crook of the base you made, where the four poles crisscross. Don't put the pole right in the middle. The bricks should be closer to the base than the bucket. (It should look like an off-centered seesaw.) Attach the pole to the base with rope. Secure it tightly enough that it doesn't slip but not so tightly you can't move it up and down.

6 Now you're ready to use your simple machine. Carefully carry the shaduf to the water source that you've chosen. To fill the bucket, pull the rope down until the bucket is submersed and filled, then let go. The weight will pull the bucket of water up! (If the water comes up too quickly, remove one of the bricks.) You can remove the bucket from the hook and carry the water to wherever you need it!

Variation: If there aren't any branches available, you can use dowels, old broom handles, or something similar. You can even make a miniature shaduf using craft sticks or small dowels, and a small plastic cup for the bucket. Make a handle out of wire and poke holes in the cup to attach it.

Supplies

- water supply, like a shallow pool, creek, or bathtub
- 4 branches, each about 3 feet long and at least 1 inch in diameter (branches that are too dry snap easily)
- several yards of rope
- 1 branch about 5 feet long and about the same diameter as the other branches
- two bricks
- several strips of old Ace bandage or duct tape, each about 2 yards long and a few inches wide
- scissors
- an S hook (you can find these at hardware stores)
- a small bucket with a handle

Time Needed

45 minutes

4 Papyrus

Papyrus, the tall marsh plant that was used to make reed boats, grew plentifully in ancient Egypt. It was so plentiful, in fact, that the papyrus plant was the hieroglyphic symbol for Lower Egypt. Egyptians used the plant in many ways: to make mats, baskets, boats, ropes, and sandals. It was even used for food, medicine, and perfume. But perhaps the most important and notable way it was used was for making paper.

Before the development of papyrus paper, ancient Egyptians often wrote on broken pottery (known as **ostraca**) or flakes of limestone. In contrast, papyrus paper (often called simply "papyrus") was durable, lightweight, and easy to roll and transport. Papyrus was first used around 4000 BCE, and it changed the world by giving people an easy way to record information. This, in turn, helped preserve a good deal of history from around the world. Some of the **Dead Sea Scrolls** were written on papyrus. Much of the New Testament from the Bible was originally written on papyrus as well.

The hieroglyph for Lower Egypt—the papyrus plant.

Papyrus is a fluffy-looking plant.

Did You Know?

The word "paper" is widely believed to come from the word "papyrus."

The texture of papyrus.

Although many papyrus **scrolls** haven't survived over time, there are still a lot of them around. What's written or drawn on these relics tells us a great deal about ancient Egyptian life. What kinds of things did the ancient Egyptians write and draw? The same kinds of things we write and draw on paper: stories and poems, letters, information on religious practices, notes about business transactions, government information, building plans, and artistic drawings or paintings. Though papyrus was fairly inexpensive to make, it wasn't cheap enough to be used for everything. Young people training to be **scribes** continued to use ostraca or stone for their lessons. People also used pottery or stone for things like lists and recipes.

Words to Know

ostraca: pieces of broken pottery or flakes of limestone written on by ancient Egyptian boys learning to read and write hieroglyphs.

Dead Sea Scrolls: ancient Hebrew scrolls discovered in caves by the Dead Sea dating from as early as the third century BCE.

scroll: a roll of papyrus.

scribe: person who read and wrote hieroglyphs.

The invention of papyrus paper helped shape the ancient Egyptian people into a great civilization. It was one of the biggest exports of ancient Egypt, and it was so important to the economy that the ancient Egyptians kept how to make it a secret. Around the tenth century CE, though, other countries brought new ways of making paper to ancient Egypt. These methods used fibers and wood pulp (ground up pieces of wood mixed with water), and this new kind of paper

A piece of a papyrus scroll.

Did You Know?

Scrolls are pieces of papyrus glued together and rolled up. In ancient Egypt, they weren't very long, typically 20 sheets or so. There are a couple of longer scrolls, though. The British Museum has one that is 133 feet long, and the Oriental Institute of Chicago has one that is 167 feet long when unrolled horizontally.

was cheaper, easier, and faster to make than papyrus. As a result, the use of papyrus died out, and so did the art of making it.

The art of making papyrus might have remained completely lost if it hadn't been for a man named Dr. Hassan Ragab. Dr. Ragab was a scientist and engineer who, in the 1960s, decided he wanted to bring papyrus back to Egypt. The papyrus plant had become extinct in modern Egypt, so his first challenge was reestablishing the plants. He did this by importing plants from Sudan and Ethiopia and starting a papyrus plantation near Cairo. Once the plant was established, his next challenge was figuring out how to make paper from it. It's impossible to know for sure how the ancient Egyptians made papyrus because they didn't write down the directions. After much experimentation, though, Dr. Ragab developed a process that he believed closely resembled the original.

The first step is to cut strips of the plant from the lower stems, which are triangular. The outer stem is removed,

Dr. Hassan Ragab worked to bring papyrus making back to Egypt.

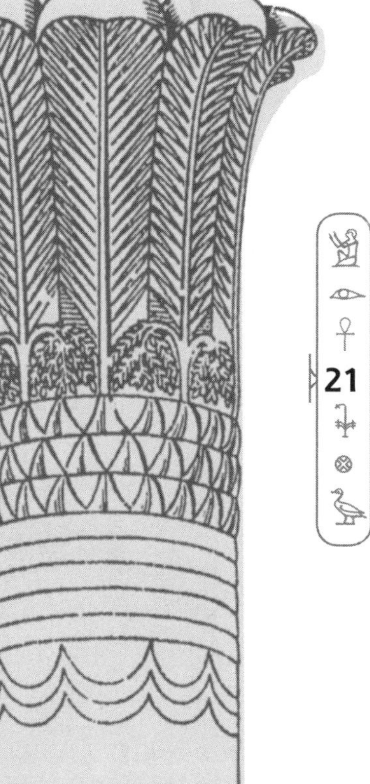

Stylized papyrus column.

Did You Know?

Papyrus was sometimes recycled and used to wrap mummies.

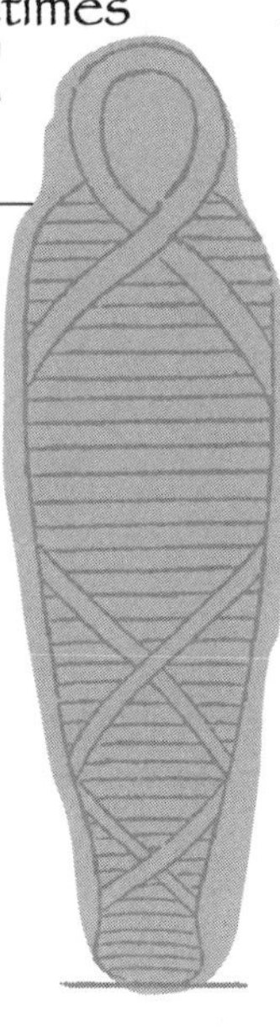

and just the pith (the soft, spongy material inside the plant) is used. The strips are pounded flat and then go through several soakings over a few days. After this, they are laid on an absorbent piece of material like cotton. (The ancient Egyptians would probably have used linen as opposed to cotton.) Strips are laid out horizontally, with each strip slightly overlapping the one above it. Then strips are laid vertically on top of the horizontal strips. Another piece of cotton and a piece of thick material are laid on top, and then everything is pressed to squeeze out any remaining water. The plant strips are squeezed and dried for 3 or 4 days. The natural gum in the pith firmly "glues" the strips together. When the piece of papyrus is finished, it has a distinctive crisscross pattern.

The Royal Library of Alexandria

The city of Alexandria, Egypt, was once a place of great learning and culture. And it was home to an amazing library called the Royal Library of Alexandria. Built by Ptolemy I Soter around 288 BCE, the library (which was made up of several buildings) was a gathering place for the greatest thinkers and home to over 500,000 books and scrolls. Scholars from all over the world met there to discuss new findings in areas such as mathematics, science, astronomy, medicine, biology, and philosophy. One of these scholars was Aristarchus of Samos, the first person to claim that the earth revolves around the sun. Another was Archimedes, the famous mathematician who calculated Pi. The Library of Alexandria was like the world's very first university!

While the Library of Alexandria thrived for over 200 years, it no longer exists. It was destroyed by a series of fires over hundreds of years, and it finally disappeared altogether in the late third century CE.

Archimedes

Make Your Own Papyrus

1 Mix the flour and the water in your pan. You can use the spoon, but your fingers will work just as well! Make sure you stir until there are no more clumps of flour. Set the pan aside.

2 Using the scissors, cut the paper into one-inch-wide strips that are roughly the same length. (Don't worry if some of the pieces are longer than others; you can trim them off later.) Put the strips of paper in the flour and water mixture and let them soak for several minutes. Make sure the pieces aren't sticking together. Move them around so each piece is covered in the mixture. While your paper soaks, spread out a piece of foil on a smooth, hard surface.

3 Next, carefully take the strips out, one at a time. Use your fingers to gently "squeegee" off the extra mixture. Lay half of the strips on the foil horizontally, making sure each piece slightly overlaps the one next to it. Lay the other half of the strips of paper on top, vertically. When you are done, you should have two layers that are perpendicular to each other.

4 Lay a piece of foil on top of your paper strips. Roll the rolling pin over the foil. Push down firmly. (Some of the flour and water mixture may seep out at the sides.) After a few minutes of rolling, slowly pull back the top piece of foil. If some of the paper strips stick to it, gently pull them off and put them back down. (You don't need to roll them again.) Put your "papyrus" sheet, still on the bottom piece of foil, out in the sun to dry. Make sure it's on a flat surface. You can also leave it inside to dry; it will just take a little longer.

5 When your paper is dry, carefully pull it away from the foil. Hold it up to the light. Notice the crisscross pattern? That's what the papyrus made by ancient Egyptians looked like! Finally, trim the edges. You're ready to write or paint on your homemade "papyrus." You can glue several sheets together and roll them up to make your very own scroll.

Supplies

- 1 cup all-purpose flour
- 2 cups water
- aluminum pan or any shallow dish
- spoon
- several sheets of unlined paper, any size—ivory or a light yellow paper will make a golden color like real papyrus
- scissors
- aluminum foil
- rolling pin

Time Needed

30 minutes

not including drying time

Make Your Own Berry Ink

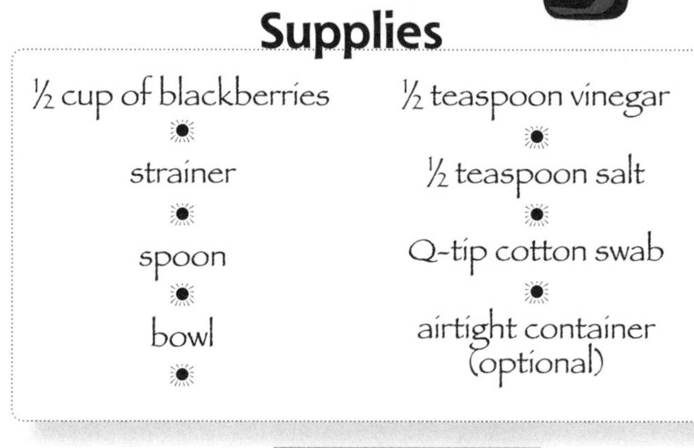

The ancient Egyptians used brightly colored minerals to make ink, but you can use blackberries to make homemade ink to use on your papyrus.

Supplies

- ½ cup of blackberries
- strainer
- spoon
- bowl
- ½ teaspoon vinegar
- ½ teaspoon salt
- Q-tip cotton swab
- airtight container (optional)

Time Needed
10 minutes

1 Pour the blackberries into the strainer. Hold the strainer over the bowl, and use the back of the spoon to force the juice out of the berries, through the strainer. When all the juice has been removed, you can throw away the pulp.

2 Add the vinegar and salt to the berry juice and mix. Your ink is now ready to use! Try using a Q-tip as a pen. Store any leftover ink in an airtight container.

Education in Ancient Egypt

As far as anyone knows, there were no formal school buildings in ancient Egypt. Children were mainly taught at home, but some became apprentices for artisans, scribes, or merchants. Boys were taught by their fathers and often followed in their fathers' professional footsteps. Girls were taught by their mothers. They learned things like cooking, sewing, dancing, and caring for younger children. There's evidence that both girls and boys were taught to read and write, although there were no textbooks. Instead, there was something called the Book of Instruction—a collection of writings, with advice on how to succeed and live a moral life. For example, here's what the Book of Instruction said about learning from others: "Do not boast of your knowledge, but seek the advice of the untutored as much as the well-educated."

5 Homes

The pyramids and temples built by ancient Egyptians are still around, but no houses are. The reason for this is very simple. The ancient Egyptians used massive stones for their pyramids and temples, but they used mudbricks, which wore down and crumbled after many years, for their homes.

Mudbricks were the perfect building material for homes in ancient Egypt, because the clay-like dirt they were made out of was plentiful. Ancient Egyptians made mudbricks in much the same way people in different parts of the world make mudbricks today. First, they collected mud in buckets made from animal skins and brought it to a work area near the home site. Next, they added straw and pebbles to strengthen the mud, which shrinks when it dries. And finally, they poured the mixture into wooden molds and put the molds in the hot sun for several days. Once the bricks had hardened, the brickmakers would turn the molds over and release them.

Mudbricks and molds.

Deir al-Madinah ruins.

Did You Know?

When an ancient Egyptian house crumbled, people often just built a new house right on top of the old one. This created little mounds called tells.

Common people (those who were not royalty or wealthy government workers) lived in simple, one- or two-bedroom, mudbrick houses of about 350 to 400 square feet (the modern family home in America is 1,500 to 2,000 square feet). There are not many of these houses around today, but there are a few in Deir al-Madinah, a village in Upper Egypt where ancient artists and craftspeople lived. Houses there were, on average, 13 by 65 feet, and built very close together, often sharing walls, like modern-day apartments or condos. A typical house had two to four rooms: a living room, hallway, and one or two sleeping areas. They also had one or two underground rooms for storage, and a small, enclosed yard. The kitchen area was frequently in the yard or in an open room in the back of the house, away from the rest of the living space because cooking indoors was so hot that it was not only uncomfortable, but dangerous. The roofs of these homes were flat, and

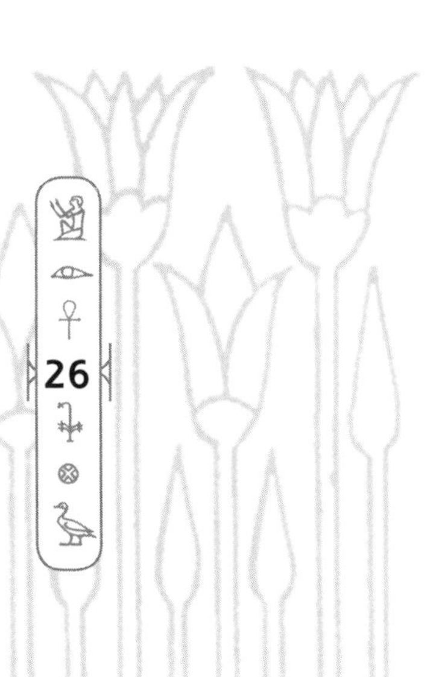

Did You Know?

The outsides of houses in ancient Egypt were painted white, because the color white helps reflect the sun's rays. Reflecting the sun kept the inside of the mudbrick homes cooler.

Ka

The ancient Egyptians believed that a person's Ka needed a house when the person died. Ka was a life force, kind of like the spiritual twin of a person. These model houses were called soul houses and provided shelter, food, clothing, furniture, and tools for a person's Ka. Soul houses were buried with the deceased.

ancient Egyptians made good use of them by sleeping there, storing their goods there, and sometimes cooking there. Much of daily living was done outdoors because of the heat.

Inside the homes, walls were painted with colorful designs or scenes from nature. Carved into the walls were small spaces for religious statues. There were few windows and those that did exist were covered with woven mats to keep out bugs and the hot sun. The floor was bare earth covered with mats. Bathrooms, if a home had one, had a toilet stool, which was a wooden bench with a hole in the middle. Underneath the stool was a bowl that could be carried outside and emptied into the streets or pits dug in the yard. Most people just went to the bathroom outdoors.

Home of a member of the wealthy class.

The houses for the wealthy classes were much bigger than those of commoners or peasants. They were two or three stories high and surrounded by lots of land, beautiful gardens, and pools. There

Household Gods

Ancient Egyptians worshipped many gods, each of whom had a special power or a certain job. Statues of certain gods or favorite gods were kept in their homes for protection. Two of the most popular household gods were **Bes** and **Taweret**.

Bes was the patron (or protector) of newborns, women in childbirth, song and dance, humor, and games. He was a strange-looking god with a dwarf's body, a bearded lion-like face, large animal ears, and a tongue that stuck out! Bes is unusual because he was the only god to be drawn mainly from the front view. Most faces in Egyptian art are drawn from the side view, as if the person or god is looking at something to the left or right of them. Because he looks so different from the other gods of ancient Egypt, some Egyptologists suspect he might have come from a different part of Africa.

Bes

Taweret was the patron god of women, children, and fertility. She had the head and body of a pregnant hippo, paws like a lion, and the back of a crocodile. These three animals are very protective of their young, and the ancient Egyptians, who lived near them, knew this well. She was often shown carrying a sa, the symbol for protection, or an **ankh**, the symbol of life. Pregnant women would often carry or wear an **amulet** in the shape of Taweret.

Taweret

were servant quarters, stables, and private water wells. Business was conducted on the bottom floors, which were usually made of stone, and families slept and socialized on the upper floors. Kitchens were outside or on the flat roof. The floors were tiled, and the walls were brightly painted. And like the more modest homes of common people, they contained special nooks and shelves for religious statues. Some estates even had small shrines. Shrines are special areas where gods are worshipped. A statue of the god might be placed in a shrine along with offerings of food or wine. Bathrooms had toilet seats made of limestone and

Did You Know?

In order to keep the Nile from flooding their homes, the ancient Egyptians built high sand dunes around their homes.

Did You Know?

There were two famous cat goddesses in ancient Egypt—**Bastet** and **Sekhmet**. Bastet was viewed as the more gentle of the two goddesses and looked like a woman with a cat's head. She was often shown with a group of kittens. Sekhmet was the goddess of battle or war and was considered to be the representation of the sun's destructive forces—burning and scorching. She was shown as a woman with a lion's head and often wore a solar disc, a round crown that represented the sun.

Bastet

Sekhmet

shallow, stone "bathtubs" where the wealthy would stand and be bathed by their servants.

Most ancient Egyptians—whether rich or poor—had very little furniture. Most people slept on the ground on mats or mattresses stuffed with straw. The wealthy had beds that were made by laying leather or wood slats horizontally across a low, wooden frame. Ancient Egyptians didn't use pillows. Instead, they rested their heads on a hard, crescent-shaped stand. Another interesting thing about some ancient Egyptian beds is that they were slightly tilted so that their feet were below their heads. (We don't know why they were built this way.) They had footboards to keep people from sliding out of bed at night!

Most of the time, people sat on the floor or on mats. But all homes had at least one low, three- or four-legged stool, which was carried from room to room, to sit on. The legs of the stools, like the legs of beds and some tables, were carved to look like animal legs. The legs of most chairs were much

Words to Know

Bes: the god of children and fun and games. Bes was a popular household god in ancient Egypt.

Taweret: the ancient Egyptian goddess of women, children, and fertility. She had the head and body of a pregnant hippo, paws like a lion, and the back of crocodile.

ankh: the hieroglyphic symbol of life.

amulets: special charms that have magic powers to protect, heal, or give the wearer a desired characteristic.

Bastet: a cat goddess who had the body of a woman and the head of a cat.

Sekhmet: a cat goddess who had the body of a woman and the head of a lion. She was the goddess of war or battle.

shorter and so the chairs were closer to the ground than those that you see today. Chairs were not common in poorer homes. Only the head of the household or honored guests sat on chairs—and chairs with armrests were strictly for the rich or powerful. In addition to stools, other common furniture items included small tables, simple oil lamps, and plenty of baskets for storage. Wooden boxes were also common for storing household goods and personal items like linens, clothes, and makeup.

Pets

Pets were very popular in ancient Egypt. Families kept birds of all sizes, baboons, and monkeys, but the most popular pets were cats and dogs.

It is believed that ancient Egyptians were the first to start keeping cats as pets. Evidence in art shows this happened around the time of the New Kingdom, the period from 1550 to 1069 BCE. Cats were very useful to the ancient Egyptians as they helped keep away the mice, rats, and snakes that hung around and ate the grain supply. Cats were adored. They were depicted in art and sculptures, given a favored spot under chairs, taken hunting, and cared for when they were sick or injured. They were even mummified when they died so that they could be buried in animal cemeteries or with their owners! By the Late Period (644–332 BCE), cats were considered sacred animals, and they were so highly worshipped at one point that harming them was punishable by death.

Ancient Egyptians didn't name their pet cats, but they did name their pet dogs. This is significant because names were considered powerful and magical. Ancient Egyptian dogs were considered a part of the family. They were used for companionship, protection, and hunting. Like cats, they were also mummified and buried with their owners. We don't know the exact breeds of dogs that lived in ancient Egypt, but the ones seen in art resemble breeds of today: greyhounds, whippets, saluki, basenji, and mastiffs. Experts believe dogs were not domesticated in ancient Egypt but brought to the country from someplace else.

Make Your Own Mudbricks

1 Take your half-gallon milk or juice carton and pinch it closed if it is opened at the top. Tape it shut. Next, fold the top down so that the carton has a squared-off top (instead of a pointy one). Tape the top to the sides. You'll probably need several pieces of tape to get it to lie flat. If your container has a pour hole, cover it with tape.

2 Lay the milk carton on its side and carefully cut off the side facing up. It's a good idea to ask an adult to help you with this because the cardboard can be hard to poke through and cut. You don't need this piece, so throw it away. Now you should have a rectangular mold.

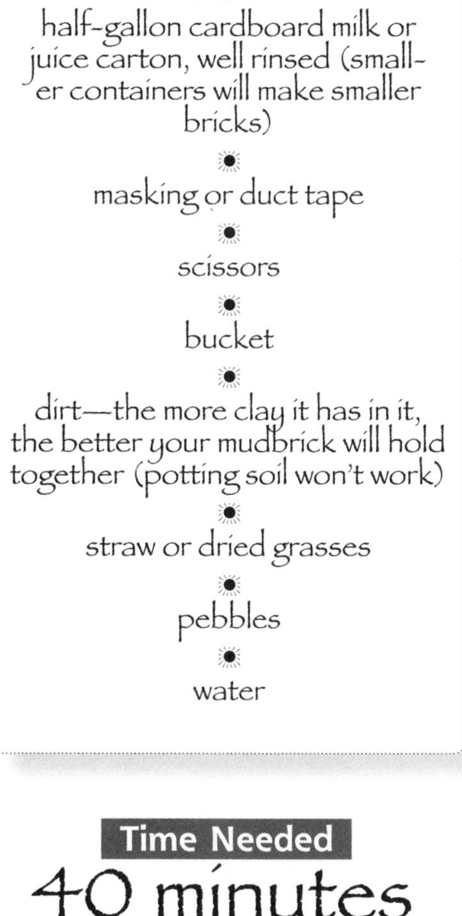

Supplies

half-gallon cardboard milk or juice carton, well rinsed (smaller containers will make smaller bricks)

masking or duct tape

scissors

bucket

dirt—the more clay it has in it, the better your mudbrick will hold together (potting soil won't work)

straw or dried grasses

pebbles

water

Time Needed

40 minutes

not including drying time

3 Put dirt, straw, and pebbles in your bucket. Mix in enough water to make the mixture wet but not soupy. It should be the consistency of brownie dough. You can use a spoon, but your hands work much better, and it's a lot more fun! How much dirt, straw, and pebbles you use depends on how big and thick a brick you'd like to make. Big bricks take longer to dry. Whether you're making a big or a small brick, you need more dirt than straw or pebbles.

4 When the mixture is ready, scoop it into your mold. Gently pat down the mud to help settle it and get rid of air pockets. Place the mold out in the sun for several days. (How long it takes for your brick to harden depends on how hot the weather is and how thick your brick is.) After the brick has dried, you can gently pull it out of the carton or cut the carton away. You will know the brick is ready when it's hard and the sides have all pulled away from the mold. Now, you're one brick closer to building an ancient Egyptian house!

Make Your Own Cat Statue

1 Take your funnel and pour the sand or pebbles through it into the bottle. This will keep your bottle/statue from tipping over. Screw the lid on tightly.

2 Crumple some newspaper into a ball that's a little bigger than a tennis ball. This will be your cat's head. Pinch and mold two more pieces of newspaper to make cat ears. Attach the ears with tape and then tape the whole head onto the top of the bottle.

3 Mix the papier-mâché as directed and dip torn strips of newspaper into the mixture. Cover the entire bottle and head with the strips. You will probably need several layers. Don't forget to cover your workspace before you begin; papier-mâché is pretty messy. Let your cat sculpture dry completely. Depending on how thick you made it and how humid the weather is, this can take from a few days to a week.

4 When your cat sculpture is dry, paint it black. You can use the white paint for details like eyes and whiskers. Add a beaded necklace for a collar if you'd like.

Supplies

- 2-liter, plastic bottle with a lid (cleaned and dried)
- 4–6 cups of sand or small pebbles
- funnel
- newspaper
- masking tape
- papier-mâché (you can buy this at any craft store or make your own by mixing 1 part water to 2 parts all-purpose flour)
- a shallow dish to hold the papier-mâché
- black and white acrylic paint
- small beaded necklace (optional)

Make Your Own

Soul House

You can make a soul house modeled after your own home or an ancient Egyptian home using air-drying dough. Note that because it dries quickly, you shouldn't mix the dough until you're ready to sculpt.

1 In your mixing bowl, blend plaster of Paris, flour, and oatmeal. Add water. (If you want to color your dough, add a few drops of food coloring to the water before you add it to the dry ingredients.)

2 Use the spoon to stir the mixture. When you can't stir it anymore, use your hands to knead it. The dough will be fairly stiff.

3 Now you're ready to sculpt your soul house. Place the dough on a sheet of wax paper. What works best is to create a bird's-eye view of a room or house. Build a low wall and then use pieces of the dough to form miniature furniture or other household items. The ancient Egyptians believed that models of things could magically become real.

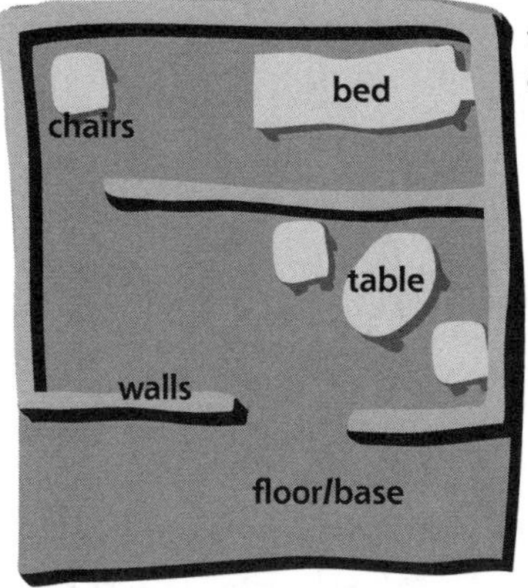

Supplies

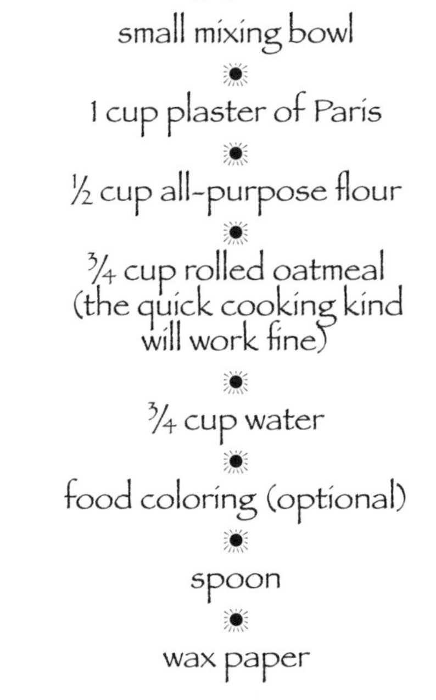
small mixing bowl

1 cup plaster of Paris

½ cup all-purpose flour

¾ cup rolled oatmeal (the quick cooking kind will work fine)

¾ cup water

food coloring (optional)

spoon

wax paper

4 When you are finished, wet your fingers and smooth out any cracks in the dough. Be sure not to get the dough too wet, though.

5 Let your soul house sit and dry. Depending on its thickness, this may take a day or two.

Note: Because the plaster of Paris sticks so well when it hardens, be sure to thoroughly wash your hands, work surface, bowl, and spoon. Dispose of any extra dough in the garbage—not the sink!

6 Bread

Ancient Egyptians led simple lives, and so it's not surprising that their diet was simple as well. They ate lots of vegetables, such as onions, leeks, lettuce, fava beans, lentils, cucumbers, and radishes. They also ate fruits, such as dates, grapes, and figs. Of course, the Nile provided plenty of fish, which ancient Egyptians usually dried in the sun. Farm animals like geese, ducks, and goats provided fresh eggs and milk. And wild game provided meat for the wealthy. Common folks ate meat, too, but it was mainly reserved for festivals or other special occasions. The most popular food and drink combination—with everyone from peasant to pharaoh—was bread and beer.

Ancient Egyptians made a variety of breads. Just like today, different people liked different types of bread. Some breads were sweet, some were airy, and some were dense. Most loaves were oval shaped, but some were triangular or cone shaped. Some loaves were even shaped to look like animals. Women were the bread bakers, and they made bread by kneading together barley or emmer wheat flour with a little bit of water, yeast, oil, and seasonings. The dough was then set aside to rise, and then it was baked. Ancient Egyptians baked their bread in dome-shaped, earthenware ovens that were about 3 feet high and heated with wood or charcoal. Ancient Egyptians didn't use sugar to sweeten

Did You Know?

There are few written recipes from ancient Egyptian times. What we know about ancient Egyptian food was learned from studying pictures in tombs or analyzing the residue left in old pottery jars.

The Downside of Making Bread in the Desert

Aside from honey and other natural sweeteners like fruit, ancient Egyptians didn't eat a lot of sweets. They had great teeth then, right? Wrong! Ancient Egyptians had terrible dental health. This was largely because sand from the desert environment would blow into their grain and get mixed into their bread. When they ate the bread the sand that had been baked into it would wear down their tooth enamel. From studying mummies we know that lots of ancient Egyptians suffered from tooth decay, painful abscesses, and gum disease. These infections may even have killed people they were so bad. While there is evidence here and there that some ancient Egyptians had fillings or other dental work done to their mouths, dentistry was not common. Most of the time, toothaches were treated with spices.

Illnesses that are common and easily treated today—like gum disease and the common cold—were mysteries to the ancient Egyptians. They believed such ailments were caused by gods or by evil spirits, and so they treated them with spells and magic, like wearing or carrying around lucky charms called amulets. Natural remedies, including garlic, coriander, cumin, castor oil, and honey were used to treat various ailments. To treat a common cold, ancient Egyptians gave the sick person breast milk from a woman who had given birth to a boy.

Ankh symbol (top) and scarab beetle (bottom) as amulets.

their bread; they used honey or dates. They also used savory spices such as salt, parsley, cumin, or coriander to give bread flavor.

You might be surprised to hear that both children and adults drank beer in ancient Egypt! It was a very common drink among both the rich and poor. It is believed that women made beer from leftover bread dough. The dough was made with barley, and beer makers would add the dough to water to make a mash, which they would set aside to ferment, and gradually change into a fizzy beer. The mash would then be strained, and flavorings would be added before pouring the beer into pottery jars. No one knows for sure what it tasted like, but it was probably sweeter and less bubbly than beer today. Both bread and beer were frequently left in tombs for the deceased as offerings or for use in the afterlife. Often, people were paid for their work in beer.

Did You Know?

Even though drinking beer was common, being drunk in public in ancient Egypt was considered very poor manners and highly frowned upon.

The people of ancient Egypt didn't have grocery stores like we have today. When they needed food and other items, they went to open markets. They had to shop for food often because of the climate. In the desert heat, food spoils quickly, and there was no way to refrigerate things. Food that wasn't eaten right away had to be preserved in some way by salting, drying, or smoking. The ancient Egyptians did not use money to obtain goods at the market. Instead, they used a **bartering system** where they traded one thing for another.

Words to Know

bartering system: a system in which people trade goods for goods rather than goods for money.

deben: a weight usually made of copper that the ancient Egyptians used in their bartering system.

When families shared a meal, they sat at low tables. Plates, bowls, and serving trays were made of pottery. Many cooking pots and pans were also made from pottery. Meals were special parts of festivals, banquets, or other parties. In addition to there being plenty of food at special events, there was entertainment in the form of dancers, acrobats, and music. Small drums, tambourines, and harps were common instruments. One thing ancient Egyptians didn't use, even during big banquets, was silverware! People ate with their fingers and cleaned their hands in bowls of water.

Did You Know?

Ancient Egyptians were fond of wine, although it was too expensive for most people to drink every day. They made fine wines, taking care to use grapes from certain vineyards and even dating the storage jugs.

Bartering in Ancient Egypt

Coins weren't introduced to ancient Egypt until the fifth century BCE. But this doesn't mean the ancient Egyptians didn't have an organized economic system—they did! They used a bartering system. A bartering system is one in which goods are traded for other goods.

To make sure trades went smoothly and were fair, people used a special weight, called a **deben**, to price things. A *deben* was usually made of copper and weighed about 3 ounces. They were frequently ring shaped, but could also be round or animal shaped. The ancient Egyptians also used other weights. For instance, 10 *kites* equaled 1 *deben*. And 10 *debens* equaled one *sep*.

When an ancient Egyptian wanted to buy something, he or she would go to the seller. Sellers would set up their tents, creating a market along the Nile to display their goods. A *deben* (or another weight) would be placed on one side of a scale, and the goods would be placed on the other side. Then the seller and buyer would agree on a fair exchange. For example, 1 *deben* of onions might have been traded for 3 *debens* of oil.

Make Your Own Bread

Ancient Egyptians made a wide variety of breads. Many used yeast, but some did not. This is a recipe for a flatbread, meaning no yeast is used, but it has other ingredients that would have been available thousands of years ago. You'll be using the oven for this activity, so ask a grown-up for help!

1 In a large mixing bowl, mix flours and salt with your hand or a spoon. Add oil and water, and keep mixing until you have a stiff dough. Add a little more water if you need to.

2 When you have a stiff dough, take it out of the bowl and put it on a lightly floured surface. Knead the dough until it's smooth, about 5 minutes. Put the dough back into the bowl, cover it with the towel, and put it in a warm place for about an hour.

3 After an hour, put the dough on a lightly floured surface, break it into about a dozen equal-sized pieces, and roll the pieces into balls. Cover the balls with a damp towel while you heat the frying pan (don't grease it!) on medium heat.

4 When the pan is heated, use your hands to flatten a ball of dough into a 6-inch circle on your lightly floured surface. Carefully pick up the dough circle, dust off any extra flour, and place it into the pan. Cook the dough for about 1 minute. Use the spatula to flip it over, and cook on the other side for about 1 minute. The bread might puff up a little, and that's okay. Cook one ball of dough at a time. You can keep those that are done in a warm place, under a towel, until you're ready to eat them.

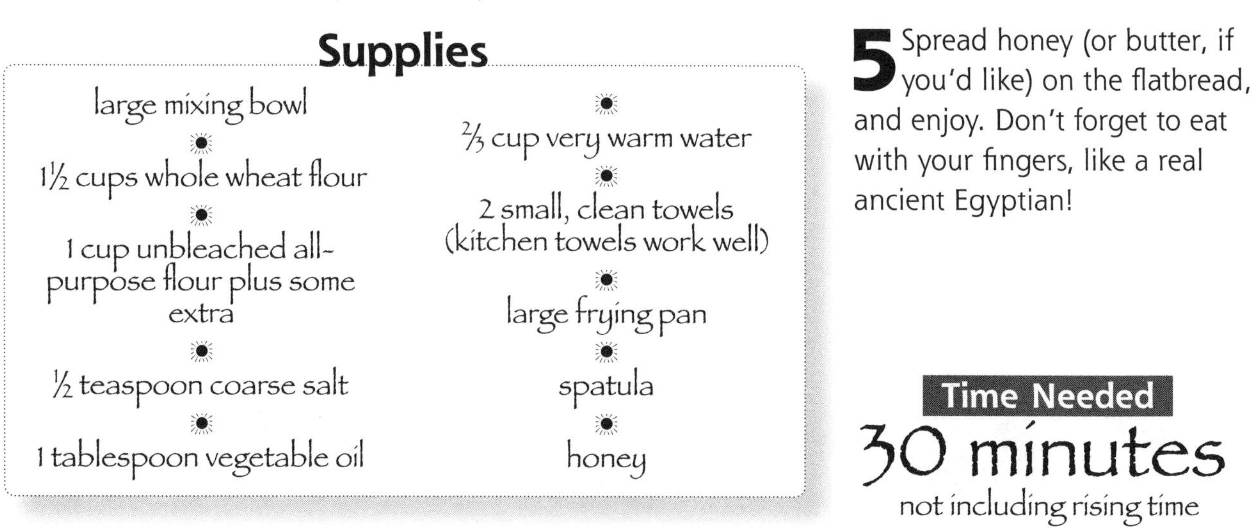

Supplies

- large mixing bowl
- 1½ cups whole wheat flour
- 1 cup unbleached all-purpose flour plus some extra
- ½ teaspoon coarse salt
- 1 tablespoon vegetable oil
- ⅔ cup very warm water
- 2 small, clean towels (kitchen towels work well)
- large frying pan
- spatula
- honey

5 Spread honey (or butter, if you'd like) on the flatbread, and enjoy. Don't forget to eat with your fingers, like a real ancient Egyptian!

Time Needed

30 minutes

not including rising time

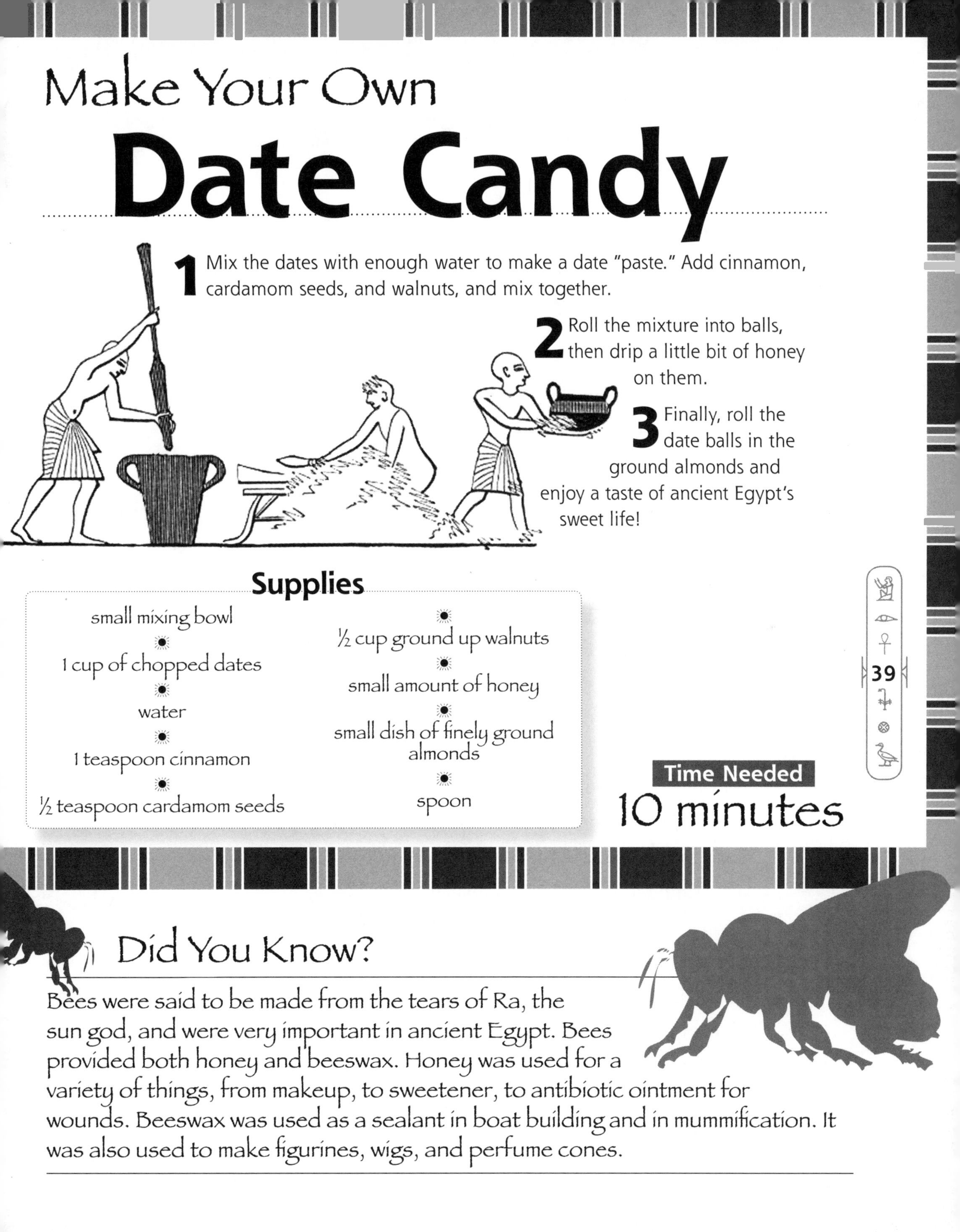

Make Your Own

Date Candy

1 Mix the dates with enough water to make a date "paste." Add cinnamon, cardamom seeds, and walnuts, and mix together.

2 Roll the mixture into balls, then drip a little bit of honey on them.

3 Finally, roll the date balls in the ground almonds and enjoy a taste of ancient Egypt's sweet life!

Supplies

- small mixing bowl
- 1 cup of chopped dates
- water
- 1 teaspoon cinnamon
- ½ teaspoon cardamom seeds
- ½ cup ground up walnuts
- small amount of honey
- small dish of finely ground almonds
- spoon

Time Needed
10 minutes

Did You Know?

Bees were said to be made from the tears of Ra, the sun god, and were very important in ancient Egypt. Bees provided both honey and beeswax. Honey was used for a variety of things, from makeup, to sweetener, to antibiotic ointment for wounds. Beeswax was used as a sealant in boat building and in mummification. It was also used to make figurines, wigs, and perfume cones.

7 Games

Children in ancient Egypt weren't that different from children nowadays. Because they lived next to the Nile River, fishing, boating, and swimming were popular pastimes. (They had to look out for alligators and hippos though!) When they weren't enjoying the water, they played games like leapfrog, which they called ***khuzza lawizza***, and tug-of-war.

Boys enjoyed rough activities, such as games that were like hockey, wrestling, or boxing, or games that involved throwing spears or sticks. One popular game was called the "Kid Is Made to Fall." To play this simple game boys would sit on the ground and try to knock over another boy as he attempted to jump over them. Girls enjoyed activities such as dancing—but they also liked to wrestle and race each other like the boys. In ancient Egyptian art, boys and girls are usually

pictured playing with their own gender. It's likely, however, that boys and girls played together.

Ancient Egyptian children had toys, too. Many of them were similar to toys we have today. Archaeologists have found models and other playthings in tombs. Models of boats and animals were made from a variety of materials: wood, bone, clay, ivory, and stone. Some toys had wheels and were pulled along with a string, while others were very elaborate with hinged mouths or other moving parts. Dolls were popular in ancient Egypt. Children or their parents made rag dolls by stuffing papyrus into a sewn figure. Ancient Egyptian kids had balls to catch and throw. There was no rubber, so balls were made by stuffing leather or wrapping strips of linen (or reeds or string) around and around and then tying the ends. Balls were painted bright colors. Children and their families probably made most toys.

Did You Know?

Dice and marble games were very popular in ancient Egypt. Ancient marbles were made of stone.

Ancient Egyptians of all ages and social classes enjoyed board games. One of the oldest is **Mancala**, a game that was invented outside of Egypt, perhaps in Ethiopia. Mancala is a game of strategy that uses a game board with holes and small stones. Today, playing pieces are often made of glass; long ago, they were made of stone, ivory, or clay, and the holes were scooped out of the ground. The object of Mancala is to move your pieces around the board, collecting as many stones as you can before your opponent clears all the stones on his or her side of the board. Other board games that were

Words to Know

khuzza lawizza: a game like leapfrog played by ancient Egyptian children.

Mancala: an ancient game that uses a game board with holes and small stones for counting.

Senet: a board game that was popular in ancient Egypt and is still enjoyed today by people all over the world.

Hounds and Jackals.

popular in ancient Egypt were Hounds and Jackals, and Mehen. Hounds and Jackals was similar to the modern-day board game of Chutes and Ladders. The board had holes and paths, and players moved their pieces around the board along these paths. Mehen was played on a one-legged table with a top that looked like a coiled snake. The snake's body was divided into squares, and players moved their pieces along these squares.

From all the ancient Egyptian drawings on tombs and in art, we know that the most popular board game in ancient Egypt was probably **Senet**. Senet was a two-player game and involved at least five game pieces that were moved around the board. One set of pieces was cone- or triangular-shaped; the other set was round. Players threw flat sticks (or knucklebones or dice) to determine

Did You Know?

Four sets of Senet were found in King Tutankhamen's tomb. King Tutankhamen is also known as King Tut. They ranged in size from miniature to the size of a small table. The table-sized one was quite fancy. It was made of ebony, ivory, and gold, and it was engraved with King Tut's name. Archaeologists believe that this fancy game board had gold or silver bolts at one time, but that they were stolen a long time ago by tomb robbers.

Did You Know?

Breaking the rules of a game was considered a serious offense. Children who cheated or broke rules were kicked or hit with sticks.

how far they moved their pieces around the board. Some ancient Egyptian Senet game boards were quite fancy, carved out of ivory or detailed with gold, but most were simple and made from wood or limestone.

No one really knows if Senet was simply a game or if it had some kind of religious significance. Some believe that the game was a sort of symbol of a person's journey through life. Senet games were often placed inside tombs, which could mean that playing the game was viewed as a way for the dead to play their way into the afterlife.

Queen Nefertari, the first wife of Rameses II, playing Senet.

Rules of Senet

Because they weren't written down, we don't really know the rules to Senet or any other ancient Egyptian games. The ancient Egyptians, like many cultures throughout history, passed down the rules to many games from generation to generation verbally. All we can do is make educated guesses based on the board, playing pieces, and drawings left behind; unless the rules are someday discovered inside a tomb we will have no way of knowing if these guesses are correct.

There are several versions of possible rules for Senet. Two men, R.C. Bell and Timothy Kendall, came up with two of the most popular ones. Bell is the author of several books on the history of board games. Kendall is an archaeologist and author of a book that studies Senet and its religious significance.

Make Your Own

Senet Game

1 With your black marker, color one side of each craft stick. Set the sticks aside. Remove the shoebox lid and cover it with paper. Secure with tape or glue. Use the marker to make 30 equal squares. There should be three rows of ten.

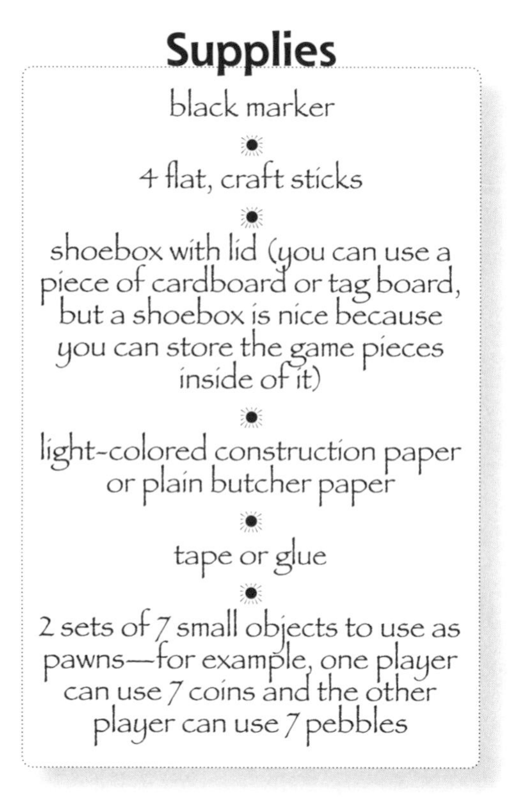

Supplies

black marker

4 flat, craft sticks

shoebox with lid (you can use a piece of cardboard or tag board, but a shoebox is nice because you can store the game pieces inside of it)

light-colored construction paper or plain butcher paper

tape or glue

2 sets of 7 small objects to use as pawns—for example, one player can use 7 coins and the other player can use 7 pebbles

2 Imagine your squares are numbered as pictured, but don't actually write the numbers on the squares. The actual game board will not have the numerals written on it as they are in this diagram, but you need to know the order to create the board with the appropriate symbols and move in the right direction during play.

3 On square 15, draw an ankh. This is the House of Rebirth.

On square 26, draw a circle. This is the House of Beauty.

On square 27, draw two wavy lines (to look like water). This is the House of Humiliation.

On square 28, draw three lines. This is the House of Three Truths.

Time Needed

30 minutes

not including playing time

1	2	3	4	5	6	7	8	9	10
20	19	18	17	16	15	14	13	12	11
21	22	23	24	25	26	27	28	29	30

On square 29, draw two lines. This is the House of Re-Atoum.
On square 30, draw one line. This is the last square. Some game boards don't mark this square with a symbol; instead it is painted a different color than the rest of the board. Feel free to mark this square however you please.

We believe ancient players moved across the board in a reverse S, starting at square 1. Before you begin playing, you might want to lightly draw a backwards S on the board so you don't forget which direction the pawns are supposed to travel. Now that your board is done and you have your sticks and pawns handy, you are ready to begin play!

To play using Kendall's rules

To begin, players put their pawns on squares 1–14: one player's pawns on all the even squares, the other player's pawns on the odd squares. Choose which player will go first. (You can do this by playing rock, paper, scissors, or by throwing the sticks to see who has a higher number of colored or non-colored sides—it's up to you!)

Player One throws the sticks. If one colored side shows, Player One may move any of his or her pawns one space. If two colored sides show, a pawn will move two spaces. If three colored sides show, a pawn moves three spaces. If four uncolored sides show, the pawn moves four spaces and the player gets to throw the sticks again. If all four colored sides show, then Player One gets to move his or her pawn five spaces.

Players may move any one of his or her pawns to an empty square OR to a square that is occupied by an unprotected pawn of his or her opponent. An unprotected pawn is one that is not next to any other pawn on the same team. If Player One's pawn lands on a square occupied by an unprotected pawn of Player Two, Player Two's pawn is moved back to where Player One's pawn started on that turn.

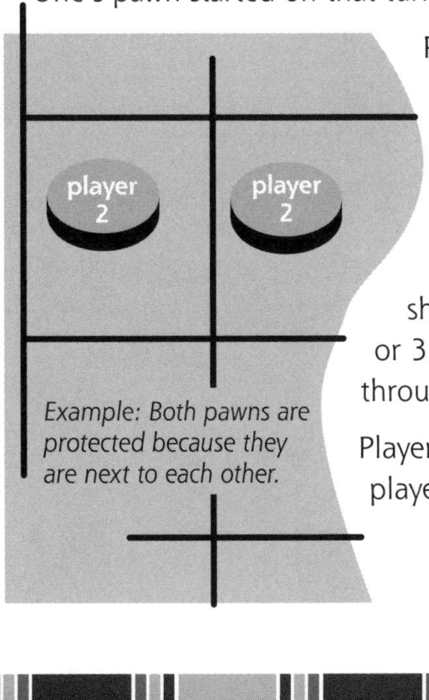

Example: Both pawns are protected because they are next to each other.

Players cannot land on a square where one of their own pawns is sitting. Only one pawn can be in a square. If a square is occupied with your own pawn, you may jump over that square or squares. You can begin or continue counting at the first open square.

If a player throws a total of either 1 or 4 colored sides, he or she gets to move a pawn and then go again. If a player throws 2 or 3, there is no extra turn. These "extra throw" rules are followed through the whole game.

Players continue to move until all their pawns are off the board. The player that achieves this first wins.

Rules on moving

As mentioned above, players cannot bump (trade places with) a protected pawn. (Remember, a protected pawn is one that has at least one matching pawn next to it.) If none of a player's pawns can move forward, then a pawn must be moved backward. If it lands on an opponent's unprotected pawn, the unprotected pawn gets to move forward to the square the other pawn came from. (A nice deal for the pawn in the back!)

Landing on the special squares

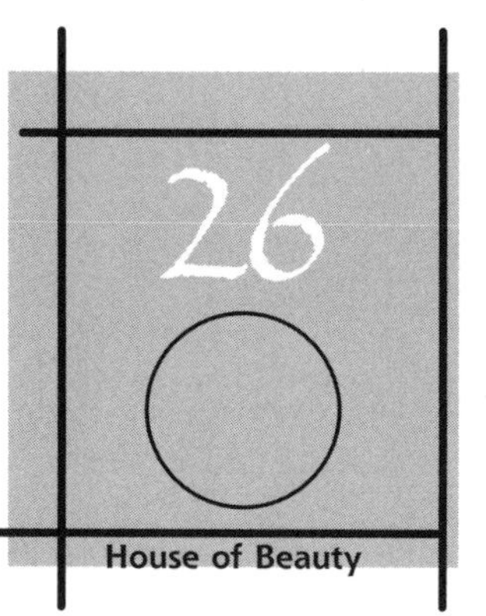

House of Beauty

Players cannot move their pawns past the House of Beauty (square 26) without landing there first. This means they must throw the exact number of colored sides to get there. After a pawn has visited the House of Beauty, it may be moved on the player's next turn.

If a pawn lands on the House of Humiliation (square 27), that player's turn is over. A pawn in the House of Humiliation is never protected, even if there are matching pawns next to it. So, if there are no other moves for a player and his pawn has to move backward, a pawn may get bumped ahead as it trades places with the attacking piece.

House of Humiliation

If a pawn lands in the House of Humiliation, no other pawn may be moved until that pawn is rescued. A pawn in the House of Humiliation may be rescued two ways: (1) It may simply be moved back to the House of Rebirth (square 15), as long as that square is not occupied by another pawn (even an unprotected pawn); or (2) It may be moved off the board with a throw of 4. In this case, after a 4 is thrown, the player's turn is over. (Note: going back to the House of Rebirth requires no throw; it's just like starting yourself over at the beginning.)

For a pawn to be moved off the board, it must first land on the last square (30). From there, any number throw can move the pawn off. The exceptions: if you are in the House of Humiliation, you must throw a 4 to move off; if you are in the House of Three Truths, you must throw a 3 to move the pawn off the board; and if you are in the House of Re-Atoum, you must throw a 2 to move the pawn off the board.

It may seem like there are a lot of rules to play Senet. But once you play a few times, you'll get the hang of it! If you want, you and your friends can also make up your own rules to play.

Tunics and Fashion

Appearances were important to ancient Egyptians. They took great care and pride in grooming and fashions. If you check out some art and drawings from ancient Egyptian times, you'll see that these fashions ranged from very simple to very fancy.

Because of the hot climate, farmers and other workers wore very little clothing. Men typically wore **kilts**, which were wraparound-style skirts that were tied, pinned, tucked in, or held up with a sash. The length of the kilts varied throughout the years. During certain years they were short, around the knee, and at other times they were longer. At some periods in history they also had pleats. Both men and women wore **tunics**. Tunics are like long T-shirts. Like other clothing, tunics and kilts were plain white and made with linen. Cotton and silk did not come along until late in ancient Egypt's history.

In addition to tunics and kilts, women wore tightly fitted dresses that were long enough to cover their ankles. A common design was the **sheath dress**, which was a

A tunic.

Did You Know?

Ancient Egyptian priests were supposed to keep their bodies shaved. They did this to stay "clean" for religious rituals. This is why priests in pictures have no hair or eyebrows.

long, tight-fitting garment that went from the ankles up to underneath a woman's breasts. They had one or two straps. Sometimes the straps covered a woman's breasts, sometimes they didn't. Ancient Egyptians were very comfortable with nudity. In fact, it wasn't unusual for women to wear sheer (see-through) dresses. Ancient Egyptian children weren't shy either; oftentimes they ran around without any clothes on.

In later years of ancient Egyptian history, dresses became more loose and flowing. They had plenty of pleats and gathers, and they draped dramatically over the shoulder. They were often decorated with jeweled pins, fancy belts, or colorful sashes—especially when people were going to festivals or parties. Animal skins (such as leopard skin) were sometimes worn, but they were usually reserved for people of high social status, like priests.

There were no such things as high-heeled shoes, tennis shoes, or boots in ancient Egypt. For the most part, people went barefoot. When they did wear shoes, most wore sandals with a toe strap, similar to the flip-flops of today. Some people, like royalty, also had sandals that looked like slippers without heels. The poor had sandals made of papyrus; the rich had sandals made of leather. Some of the sandals found

Words to Know

kilt: a wraparound-style skirt either tied, pinned, tucked in, or held up with a sash.

tunic: a piece of clothing worn by both men and women in ancient Egypt. Tunics looked like long T-shirts.

sheath dress: a dress worn by ancient Egyptian women.

Khufu: an ancient Egyptian king who ruled from 2589 to 2566 BCE and built the Great Pyramid at Giza.

***nemes*:** a head covering that ancient Egyptian royalty wore.

Tutankhamen (King Tut): A king who ruled from 1336 to1327 BCE. His tomb is famous because it was found much later than most and was the only one *not* robbed in modern times.

diadem: a type of headband worn by ancient Egyptians.

What Is the Sphinx Wearing?

The Great Sphinx is a famous limestone sculpture of a creature that has the body of a crouching lion and the head of **King Khufu**. Have you ever seen photos of the Sphinx and wondered what it's wearing on its head? The special headdress is called a ***nemes***. This is a striped piece of cloth that is pulled tight across a person's forehead and tied behind their head while the sides are left to hang by their face. It is what royalty used to cover their heads when they weren't wearing crowns, as it was tradition for royalty not to show their natural hair. There are many works of art, in addition to the Great Sphinx, that show a *nemes*. King Tut's funeral mask is one example.

in the tomb of **Tutankhamen** were covered in gems and gold sequins!

Ancient Egyptian men usually wore their hair short and straight, but curls were also somewhat popular. Women had many hairstyles. In the Old Kingdom, the fashion was a short, chin-length bob. In the New Kingdom, the style was long hair. Women would often weave ribbons or flowers in their hair. They also used hair extensions, which were "glued" on with beeswax or woven in, because thick hair was considered an attractive feature. Women frequently used **diadems** to decorate or hold back their hair. Sometimes, hair was put into tiny braids or ringlets that were pulled over to hang from one side of the head. Both men and women sometimes shaved their heads. This was probably done to keep cool or avoid lice.

King Tut's gold funeral mask. Notice the *nemes* on his head.

Did You Know?

Ancient Egyptian men didn't usually have mustaches or beards. The stiff, straight beards you see on statues and in pictures are drawings of fake facial hair. For reasons we don't know, these fake beards were usually blue.

Words to Know

henna: the tree or the dye made from the tree used by the ancient Egyptians to make cosmetics, as well as skin and hair dye.

side-lock of youth: an S-shaped curl that children in ancient Egypt wore on the side of their heads.

Women did not walk around bald, though. They wore wigs made of human hair, wool, or vegetable fibers. Wigs were also popular with men and children. People had different wigs for different occasions, and they took great care of them. Like many other things, wigs were left inside tombs for use in the afterlife.

Ancient Egyptian children had a special hair-

Make Your Own Tunic

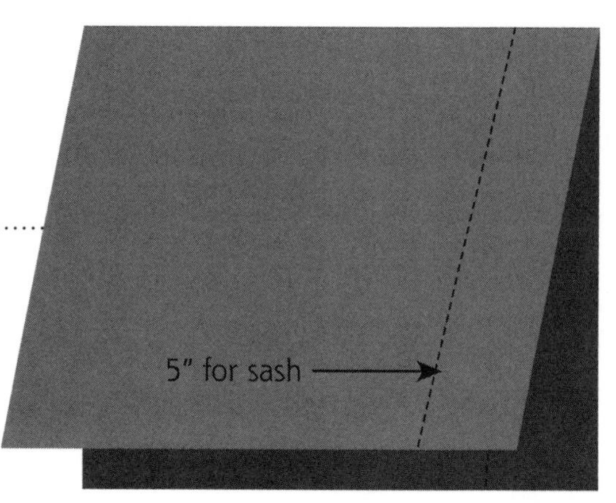

1 To figure out exactly how much fabric you need, measure from your shoulders to your knees and then multiply that length by two. Lay your material flat, then fold the material in half, width-wise. (If you plan to use the same material to make the sash, cut a strip about 5 inches wide off one of the sides. Don't cut at the fold or your sash will be too short!)

2 Cut a "T" shape out of your material as shown in the illustration. In the middle of the top of the "T," cut out a small half-oval. This will be your neck hole.

Supplies

- about 2 ½ to 3 yards of muslin or similar material, like an old, white sheet
- scissors
- 12 medium-sized safety pins OR fabric glue
- fabric paint, sequins, beads (optional)
- 2 yards of craft rope OR a strip of material to use as a sash

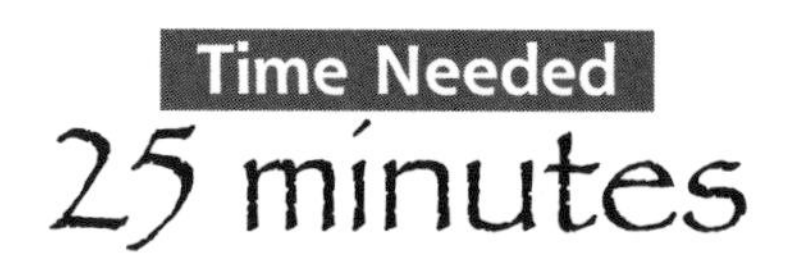

Time Needed
25 minutes

style. Until they became teenagers, both boys and girls shaved or cut all of their hair very short except for one long lock. This lock, on the side of the head, was curled like an "S." It was called the **side-lock of youth**.

Did You Know?

People sometimes used **henna** (a dye made from the henna tree) to color their hair red.

3 Using the safety pins or fabric glue, secure the sides of the tunic and the underside of each sleeve. (You can also use a sewing machine to sew up these seams.)

4 Turn the tunic inside out so that the pins or glue are not showing.

5 If you'd like, you can decorate your tunic with fabric paint or by gluing on sequins. To make a fringe, carefully cut tiny slits (about 3 inches long) along the bottom of the tunic.

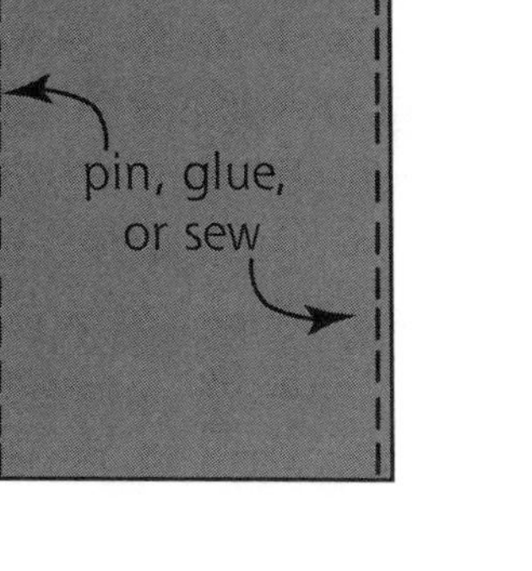

6 Add a rope or your sash around your waist and you're ready to spend the day in typical ancient Egyptian style!

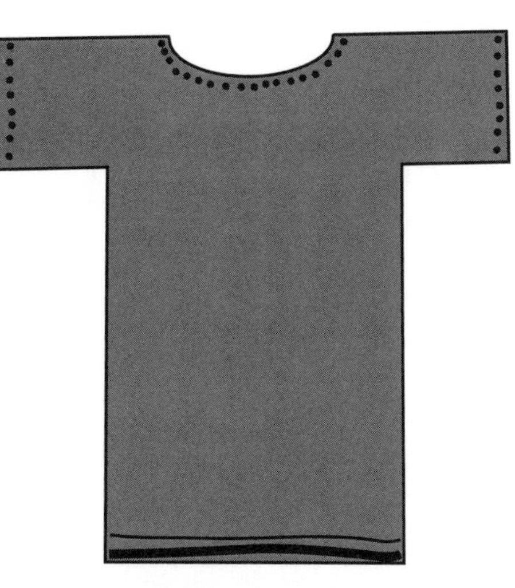

Did You Know?

For underwear, ancient Egyptians wore triangular loincloths.

Make Your Own
King Tut Sandals

Supplies

newspaper

an old or inexpensive pair of thong-style sandals (flip-flops)—the wider the top strap is, the better

gold spray paint (a small can is enough)

glue

sequins and glitter

1 Spread your newspaper out on a flat surface. You'll want to make sure it's in an area that is outside or has windows.

2 Lay your sandals in the middle of the newspaper, and, following the directions on the spray paint can, paint the tops and sides of the sandals. When they're dry, turn them over and spray paint the bottoms of the sandals, too.

3 Next, glue sequins and glitter onto your "gold" sandals.

4 Let the glue dry, and then slip your feet into a pair of sandals fit for a king or queen!

Time Needed

15 minutes

not including drying time

Make Your Own
Nemes

Supplies

striped material, about 1 yard wide and 1 yard long

safety pin

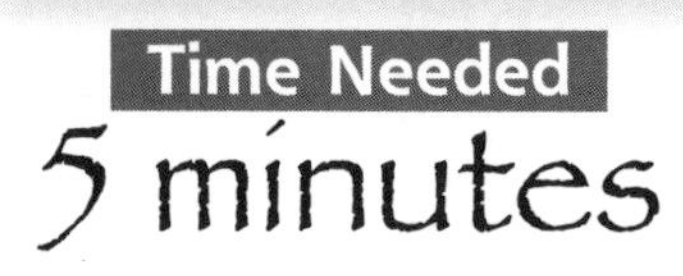

Time Needed

5 minutes

1 Place the material flat against your forehead.

2 Pull the material behind your head (over your ears) and secure it with a safety pin (be very careful not to poke yourself). Now just let the rest of the material fall on your shoulders.

9 Jewelry

Ancient Egyptian clothes may have been plain, but their jewelry was anything but plain. Colorful and highly detailed, jewelry from Egypt was—and still is—very popular.

We don't know if ancient Egyptians wore jewelry simply for decoration or for religious or protective reasons. But since we know that ancient Egyptians took pride in their appearance and included jewelry in their tombs for use in the afterlife, it was likely a combination of the two. Regardless of why they wore jewelry, we know that both ancient Egyptian men and women wore lots of it.

One of the most popular pieces of jewelry was a beaded **wesekh** collar. Typically these were quite intricate, containing hundreds or even thousands of beads. They were large, too, covering wearers from the bottom of their necks to the middle of their chests. These collars are frequently pictured in art.

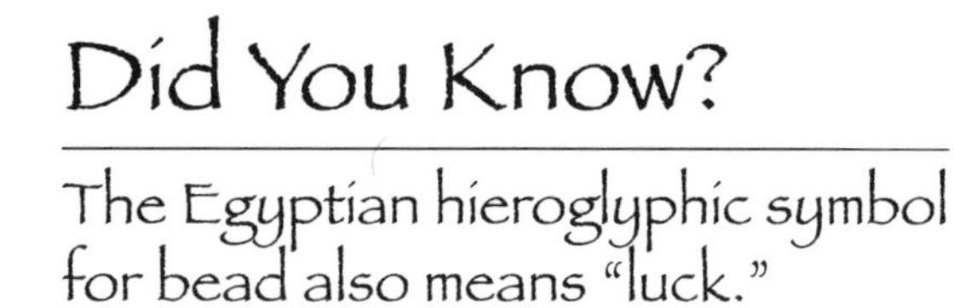

Did You Know?

The Egyptian hieroglyphic symbol for bead also means "luck."

The ancient Egyptians also wore necklaces and pendants, rings, anklets, beaded belts, earrings, bracelets, armbands, headbands (called diadems), and hair combs.

Ancient Egyptians made jewelry from many natural materials: copper, gold, silver, electrum (gold mixed with silver), bones, shells, clay beads, and colorful rocks. Gemstones used in ancient Egyptian jewelry included carnelian, turquoise, garnets, and lapis lazuli. Lapis lazuli was especially prized and was imported from what is now the country of Afghanistan. Today, some of these stones are considered semiprecious, but they may not have been in ancient times.

Egyptian necklace of glass and faience beads.

Whether or not a material is considered valuable depends, in part, on how easy it is to obtain. For instance, silver, at one time in ancient Egyptian history, was more valuable than gold because it was harder to come by.

Two other materials ancient Egyptians used to make jewelry were **faience** and glass. Ancient Egyptian faience was made primarily of ground-up quartz; water, natron (a kind of salt), and coloring were added to make a paste, which was then molded into the desired shape, fired, and glazed. Faience was typically a blue-green color, though crafters eventually figured out how to make other colors. Faience beads (and sculptures) were popular in ancient Egypt.

Glass, which forms naturally when rocks are struck by lightning or glazed by lava, has always been around. There's some debate about how, when, and where people discovered how to make glass on their own. Many experts believe Egyptians and Mesopotamians discovered how to make it around the same time,

Words to Know

wesekh: a wide, beaded collar and one of the most popular items of jewelry in ancient Egypt.

faience: a glazed, non-clay ceramic material the Egyptians used to make beads, jars, art, and amulets.

The Gemstones of Ancient Egypt

Egyptian jewelry was very colorful. Here are descriptions of gemstones that were often used.

carnelian: a type of quartz that ranges from brownish-red to deep red.
turquoise: a mineral that's greenish blue to sky blue.
garnet: a crystal that can be red, purple, orange, yellow, green, brown, or black.
lapis lazuli: a stone that's deep blue with violet or greenish tints.
amethyst: a quartz that is various shades of purple.

somewhere between 3500 and 2500 BCE. Glass beads were used in ancient Egypt to mimic the look of gemstones. The Egyptians created their beads with a technique called core forming. Using this technique, glass artists made a mold and put it on a rod. Next, they dipped the mold and rod into heated glass or trailed heated glass along the top until they had the desired thickness and design. Artists then carefully cooled their glass in a process called annealing.

The ancient Egyptians were very good at making beads of glass and faience; their beads were valuable and traded throughout the ancient world.

Did You Know?

Natural glass formed from volcanic action is called obsidian. Egyptians used it in their jewelry making, too. They imported it from other parts of the world, such as the country we now call Turkey.

Did You Know?

Ancient Egyptians were amazing jewelers. Fortunately, much of their work has survived despite tomb robbers. One of the biggest personal collections of jewelry was found in the tomb of King Tut.

Make Your Own Wesekh Collar

1 Cut your wire into two 24-inch-long pieces. These will be your top and bottom wires. Set these aside as you'll need them later. Now, cut seven 3-inch pieces of wire. We'll call these pieces "spokes."

2 At the top of each spoke, bend the wire so there is a tiny loop. Slide six beads onto the wire. When you're done, carefully bend the wire at the other end so there is a loop at that end, too. Pliers will make this job easier, but you should be able to do it with your hands. The loops just have to be big enough to keep the beads from falling off.

3 After all the spokes are finished, choose one to be your centerpiece and slide it onto one of the long pieces of wire. Let the spoke dangle while you add five beads to the long wire on each side of the spoke.

4 Add another spoke on each side, then five beads next to the spokes, like before. Keep adding beads and spokes until all the spokes have been used.

5 When you're done, carefully lay the wire down on a flat surface. Slide the second piece of long wire through the bottom loop of the spoke on the left. Add six beads.

6 Slide the wire through the bottom loop of the next spoke. Add six more beads. Continue to slide the wire and add beads until the wire has gone through the bottom loops of each spoke. Twist the wire around the end spokes to hold the pieces together; use pliers (if you're using them) to make a tight knot and to flatten the wire. Cut off the extra wire.

7 Bend the top wire to make a circle. To make a simple clasp, bend the ends of the wire to make a "C" shape and a backwards "C" shape.

Supplies

2 yards of 20-gauge copper wire (you can use string, yarn, jewelry wire, or aluminum wire, but copper has a nice golden color and can be cut and bent without using special tools)

scissors

approximately 120 plastic beads (6 by 9 mm) of any color or style

pliers (optional)

Time Needed

40 minutes

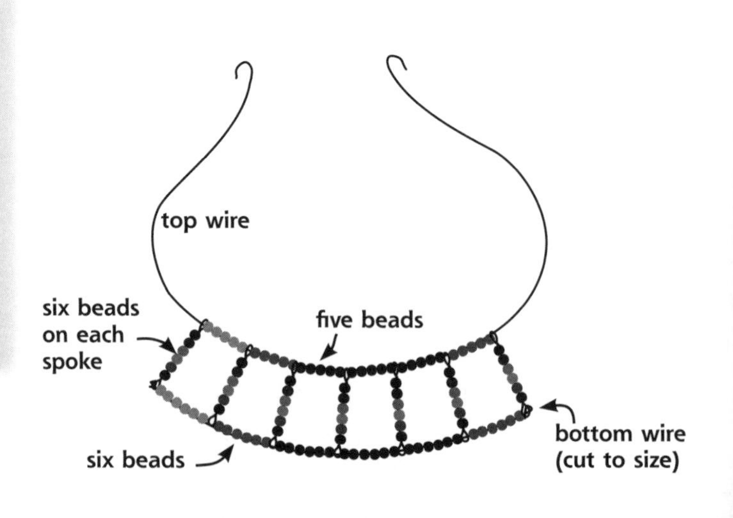

Variation: Ancient Egyptian *wesekh* collars usually used many more beads than the necklace described here. If you want, you can make more spokes with more beads. If you do this, you'll want to put only one or two beads between the loops. You can use a different size or type of bead if you'd like. You can find beads that look like glass, crystals, or gemstones at craft or bead shops. You can even make your own paper beads with the instructions below.

Make Your Own Paper Beads

1 On the white side of your scrapbooking paper, draw a rectangle that is 4 inches tall and 10 inches long. It can be less than 10 inches long if the paper isn't that wide.

2 At the top of the rectangle, use your ruler to make marks that are 1 inch apart. Do the same thing along the bottom of the rectangle.

3 Starting in a top corner, use the ruler to make a diagonal line down to the first bottom mark. Continue making diagonal lines from mark to mark. When you are done, your rectangle will be divided into 20 triangles. Cut out the triangles.

4 One at a time, roll the triangles around the middle of the pencil. Start with the fat end. (It's kind of like rolling up a crescent roll!) When it's rolled up, use a dab of glue to secure the tip of the triangle. This is your paper bead!

5 Slide the bead off the pencil and let the glue dry. Use the rest of the triangles to make more beads. The paper in different colors and designs will give you a variety of beads.

6 Once the glue is dry, snip the ends of the beads to even them out. Spray the paper beads with clear spray paint if you'd like, and allow them to dry. Now, you're ready to string your beads into a colorful necklace or bracelet.

Supplies

several sheets of scrapbooking paper in a variety of designs and colors (construction paper will work, too, but regular paper and wrapping paper are too lightweight)

pencil

ruler

scissors

glue

clear glossy spray paint (optional)

Time Needed

20 minutes

not including drying time

10 Amulets

The ancient Egyptians believed the world was filled with evil forces that caused injury, disease, natural disasters, and death. The ancient Egyptians also believed they could protect themselves from these dangers by wearing or carrying amulets. Amulets are special charms that people believe have magical powers to protect, heal, or provide the wearer with a desired characteristic.

Ancient Egyptian amulets came in a huge variety of styles, shapes, and sizes. Many resembled everyday things like frogs, stairs, serpent heads, fingers, legs, fish, hearts, and ladders. Each was made and used for a particular purpose. For instance, a fish amulet might be worn to protect the wearer from drowning. A heart amulet might have been worn to protect the wearer's heart. (Ancient Egyptian heart amulets were shaped like *real* hearts!) The djed is an amulet that looks like a

A winged scarab.

Did You Know?

The making and selling of amulets was a major industry in ancient Egypt.

The Book of the Dead

The Book of the Dead is a collection of spells, formulas, and magical texts and illustrations, written on papyrus, that ancient Egyptians used as a guidebook to the afterlife and funeral rituals. Because the Book of the Dead was usually put in coffins or wrapped in mummies, we have many copies of the book to study today.

Anubis weighs the heart of Ani (man with his wife bowing to the gods), against Ma'at's feather of truth, and Thoth records the event. Ammit the devourer waits patiently.

There are about 200 texts in the Book of the Dead. Some texts give instructions for rituals used in preparing a body for burial, such as the Opening of the Mouth. This was an important step in assuring a mummy could "eat" and "speak" in the afterlife. Other texts offer advice and spells for the journey into the afterlife. For example, chapter 6 contains a spell used to ensure that ***shabti*** would perform the work of the deceased. Chapter 125 explains how **Osiris** and 42 judges would judge the deceased and how **Ma'at** would weigh the heart of the deceased. There is even a spell to help keep the deceased's heart from betraying him or her at Osiris's court. It reads, in part, "O my heart which I had from my mother! Do not stand up as a witness against me in the judgment hall . . . do not tell them what I have really done!"

spine and was worn to protect that part of the body. Other amulets might be worn because the wearer wanted to have a certain characteristic, like the speed or strength of a certain animal. Amulets that symbolized gods and goddesses were also worn.

Everyone, young and old, wore amulets. Even babies wore amulets on necklaces, bracelets,

Did You Know?

Though there are reports of people living much longer, the average life expectancy for the ancient Egyptian was around 40 years.

Did You Know?

The gold collar we often see in Egyptian art was also an amulet. At first it was used in funerals to aid and protect the deceased. Later on, it became popular with the living.

or anklets for protection. And amulets weren't only for the living; the dead had them, too. Amulets were placed inside tombs and even tucked inside the layers of wraps of mummies. This wasn't done carelessly. The way amulets were made, the materials used to make them, and even where they were worn (or placed on the body) was serious business. This information was kept in the Book of the Dead.

Amulets were very important in ancient Egyptian medicine. Other forms of "magic" were frequently used in medicine as well. For instance, a scorpion bite (common in the desert) might be treated with an incantation or a spell. There were, of course, other remedies for injury, illness, and pain. An ancient Egyptian priest-physician could treat such things with herbs or foods such as garlic and onions. They also treated injuries with bandages and splints.

The kinds of illnesses ancient Egyptians suffered from were not much different from the ones we deal with today. They had colds, flu, headaches, upset stomachs, sore throats, and pneumonia. They had diseases such as cancer, malaria, bubonic plague, smallpox, measles, and cholera. They also suffered terribly from an eye infection called trachoma. Trachoma can cause blindness and is still a problem in Egypt and other parts of the world due to poor diet and sanitation.

Words to Know

***shabti*:** small, mummy-like figures found inside tombs. It was the *shabti's* responsibility to do any necessary work of the deceased. They were also called *ushabti* or *shawabti*.

Osiris: the god of the underworld and husband of Isis. Ancient Egyptians believed he sat on a throne and judged the deceased as they entered the afterlife.

Ma'at: the goddess and concept of truth, justice, and order.

dung beetle: a beetle considered the symbol of rebirth because it "magically" appeared from dung. The ancient Egyptians didn't know that dung beetles laid their eggs in dung.

Four Common Amulets

The ancient Egyptians had many amulets. Here are four of the most common ones.

ankh: Worn for everlasting life. It is probably one of most widely recognized symbols of ancient Egypt, as it was also the hieroglyphic symbol for life.

udjat: Also called the "eye of Horus" or the "sacred eye," it was worn for health and overall protection. According to myth, it represents the eye of the god Horus that was torn out in a fight with his evil uncle and then magically restored.

scarab: Worn for the resurrection or rebirth after death, the scarab is another widely recognized amulet. It honored the **dung beetle**. The way dung beetles roll a ball of dung across the ground was thought to represent the sun moving across the sky.

djed: Worn to protect the back and to represent stability. According to myth, it represents the backbone of Osiris, god of the underworld.

What we know about medicine in ancient Egypt comes from papyrus scrolls that have been salvaged. There are many medical papyri, but two are particularly significant and are named for the modern men who recognized them as such. The Edwin Smith papyrus tells us about how wounds were treated. The Ebers papyrus tells us about the spells used in medical care and contains descriptions of the heart and mental disorders such as depression. Both are the oldest medical papers known to exist.

Did You Know?

Not all amulets were worn for protection. Some were worn simply for good luck or fortune. It was like carrying a lucky penny or rubbing a rabbit's foot!

Make Your Own Amulet

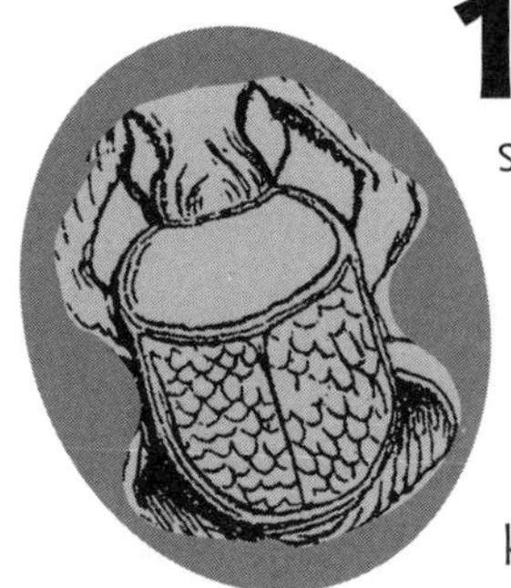

1 In the bowl, combine your sawdust and flour with just enough water to make the mixture stiff but pliable. This dough should be neither soupy nor crumbly. Add the water slowly and keep kneading the dough until it has an elastic consistency. This may take a while.

2 Take the dough out of the bowl and put it on your newspaper or wax paper. Mold your dough into any shape of amulet you want. Think about what kind of protection or characteristic you'd like to have. If you want to be good at schoolwork, you could make a pencil. If you want to be able to run faster, you could make a cheetah. If you get colds a lot, you could make a nose. Try to think of something that would be meaningful to you. Use your imagination!

Supplies

2 cups fine sawdust (ask a hardware store or lumberyard if they have some you can have—remove any small bits of wood or splinters since you'll be using your hands to mix it)

1 cup all-purpose flour

water

bowl or bucket

newspaper or wax paper

sandpaper (optional)

acrylic paint (optional)

3 If you want to wear your amulet, poke a hole in it or mold it into a bracelet.

4 Place your amulet in the sun to dry. After several days, your amulet should be very hard. You can use sandpaper to smooth it and paint to decorate it. To give it a shiny look, you can also spray it with gloss spray.

Time Needed

25 minutes

not including drying time

Kohl and Perfume

11

When people think of ancient Egypt, one image that is likely to pop into their minds is beautiful, kohl-painted eyes. Kohl is the dark powder used by ancient Egyptians to dramatically outline their eyes.

Kohl was made from ground up galena, a silver-gray mineral. People applied kohl with a special stick with a rounded end, called a cosmetic spoon, or with their fingers. The stick was dipped in water or oil, along with the kohl, so that the makeup would go on more smoothly. Kohl was worn by both men and women, young and old, rich and poor. Like other cosmetics in ancient Egypt, it was used for both beauty and health. Kohl helped protect the eyes from the glare of the sun and may have prevented or treated eye infections.

Did You Know?

The ancient Egyptians used polished silver and copper as mirrors. Other personal grooming items included tweezers, razors, and combs.

Kohl Pots

Because everyone wore kohl, numerous kohl pots from ancient Egypt have been found. Kohl pots were made out of clay, faience, and glass, and came in many shapes and sizes. Some were small and had lids, some looked like tiny jars or vases, and others were shaped like gods or animals. A popular animal shape for kohl pots was the monkey. Although they weren't native animals, monkeys were common in ancient Egypt and may have been kept as pets.

Sometimes, eyes painted with kohl are described as cat eyes. The idea that ancient Egyptians might have been trying to imitate the cat isn't surprising, since the cat was so important to them. Perhaps the design itself was another amulet they wore to protect themselves.

Eye makeup wasn't the only cosmetic used by ancient Egyptians. They used henna (a dye that comes from the henna plant) to color their hair, decorate their bodies, and dye their fingernails yellow and orange. They made rouge and lipstick from ground red ochre, a clay mineral. And they also made creams and lotions from animal or vegetable oils to soothe their skin in the harsh climate.

Ancient Egyptian perfumes were highly prized throughout the ancient world. Unlike today's perfumes, which are alcohol based, the perfumes of the ancient Egyptians were oil based. Rather than a liquid that is sprayed on, perfumes were solid and were rubbed onto the skin. Ancient Egyptians made perfumes with all kinds of essential oils made from local and imported plants, including lilies, roses,

Did You Know?

Cleanliness was considered very important to ancient Egyptians. They bathed frequently and used a soap made of ash, scented oils, animal or vegetable oils, or alkaline salts that could be lathered up.

Tattoos

Tattoos are made by injecting ink into skin. Unlike henna designs or other forms of makeup, they are permanent body art. From what we can tell from art and mummies, tattoos have been around for a very long time. For example, the mummy Amunet (a priestess) has them, and there are pictures of Queen Nefertiti with a tattoo on her arm.

Plenty of cultures all over the world use tattoos for a variety of reasons. But like many things, we can only guess at their significance in ancient Egypt. Given their use of amulets and spells, the ancient Egyptians probably believed tattoos had protective or other magical powers. What we do know is that tattoos appear to be something only females had. We also know that, at least early on, tattoos were not pictures but dashes, dots, lozenges (diamond shapes), and other geometric shapes. The first known tattoos of an image are from pictures of dancers who had the god Bes tattooed on their thighs.

cinnamon, henna, spikenard, ginger, and sandalwood. They also used plant parts, such as the resin of frankincense and myrrh. Ancient perfume makers obtained essential oils by squeezing plants to extract juices and oils. Then they added these oils to wax, animal fats, and other ingredients to make scents. These scents were probably stronger and different than the ones we find pleasing today.

Good-smelling wood, bark, spices, oil, and resin were also burned or left on hot coals to smolder, creating pleasant smells. These aromatic smells are called incense. Incense was thought to have special healing powers and was frequently used in temple rituals or during meditation in ancient Egypt. It was also used to cover unpleasant smells like cooking, animal sacrifices, or decaying bodies. (It took 70 days to mummify a body!) Today, many people use incense just because they like the smell. Some religions continue to use it in ceremonies as well.

Did You Know?

Perfumes were found in King Tut's tomb. Some still had their smell after having been buried for thousands of years!

A perfume spoon.

Make Your Own

Kohl Pot

1 Soak the shredded crepe paper in warm water for several hours, or until the paper is very soft.

2 Pour off any extra water and add ½ cup flour. Mix with your hands. Once the dough is thoroughly mixed, remove it from the bowl and place it on a piece of wax paper. Use the extra flour to lightly flour the surface of the wax paper.

3 Knead the dough until it looks and feels like pie crust dough.

4 Mold the crepe paper dough over your baby food jar. Don't put clay on the bottom of the jar, though! And don't put clay around the top where the lid screws on, either. Otherwise, you won't be able to put the lid on your kohl pot.

5 After you've covered the jar, cover the top of the lid. Don't put the lid on the jar yet—let the jar and lid air dry separately.

Supplies

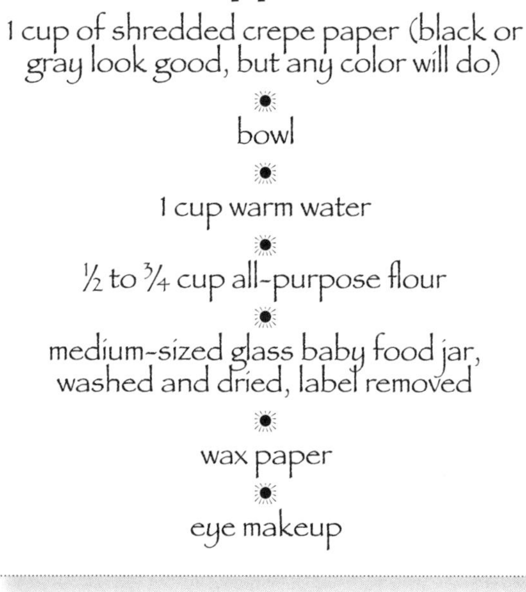

1 cup of shredded crepe paper (black or gray look good, but any color will do)

bowl

1 cup warm water

½ to ¾ cup all-purpose flour

medium-sized glass baby food jar, washed and dried, label removed

wax paper

eye makeup

6 Once they're dry, grind up the eye make-up and put it into your kohl pot. You can use the brush that came with the makeup, a cotton swab, or your finger to apply it. Now you can be ready at a moment's notice for an ancient Egyptian party!

Time Needed

20 minutes

not including soaking and drying time

Make Your Own
Perfume

This activity involves using a stove, so make sure you ask an adult for help.

You can buy the ingredients to make your own perfume at most craft stores or stores that sell aromatherapy products. Look in the candle- or soap-making section.

beeswax

glass bowl

pot of boiling water

1 Fill your pot with tap water and bring it to a boil. Once the water is boiling, have an adult carefully place the glass bowl on top of the pot so that it is sitting on the rim of the pot but not touching the water. Turn off the stove but don't remove the pot.

2 Put the beeswax in the glass bowl and let it melt. Stir it occasionally with the craft stick. It might take several minutes for the beeswax to melt completely.

3 Once the wax has melted, add the sweet almond oil. Stir until the wax and oil are completely mixed. Add the distilled water and mix.

Supplies

pot to boil water

glass bowl

2 tablespoons grated beeswax

2 tablespoons sweet almond oil

1 tablespoon distilled water

1 to 2 teaspoons essential oil (choose one scent or experiment with mixing scents)

wooden craft stick

small glass baby food jar with lid, washed and dried, label removed

4 Cool the mixture slightly and then add your essential oil. Carefully pour the mixture into the baby food jar. Let it cool and harden before putting the lid on the jar.

5 Ancient Egyptians made beautiful and elaborate perfume bottles. If you'd like, you can decorate your perfume jar using paint, gold trim, or sequins.

6 Enjoy the new perfume you personally designed by rubbing some of it on your body!

Royal Crook and Flail

Imagine being in charge of everybody and everything around you. What you want, you get. What you say, people do. Everyone follows your rules, and citizens and servants alike wait on you hand and foot. This is what it was like for the kings of ancient Egypt. It's called **absolute power**.

Ancient Egyptians believed their kings, called pharaohs, were embodiments of the god **Horus**, a falcon god and the son of Osiris, the head of the **underworld**. In other words, they thought their kings *were* gods and could communicate with other gods. Kings were not elected. The job was usually passed down from father to son when the father died. But *usually* doesn't mean always. A few rulers became pharaohs when they married into the royal family or took over for a king who was too young to rule.

Horus

Kings held their position until their deaths and were typically men. There were, however, at least four women that we know of who ruled ancient Egypt. Surprisingly enough, all rulers of ancient Egypt were called pharaohs, even those who were women! The title of "queen" only referred to the mothers or wives of kings.

Did You Know?

The word *pharaoh* is a Greek word that is based on an ancient Egyptian word (*per-aa*) that meant "great house." Long ago, the word referred not to the person who ran things but to the place where he or she lived.

Being king meant having power and tremendous resources. They lived with their families in big, beautiful homes filled with gold, art, and jewelry, and their land was covered in beautiful gardens and ponds. Kings had the best food and the best entertainment available. And they had secretaries, wardrobe attendants, hairdressers, beauticians, personal cooks, and a host of other servants waiting on their every need and desire. Festivals and all offerings to the gods were made in their name and honor.

Being king was not a cakewalk, however. Kings were expected to be physically strong and good hunters and soldiers. It was their job to protect Egypt from its enemies, which included the Libyans and Nubians. They were in charge of running the entire government and guiding the governors and all other important officials. This required a lot of thought and organization. As gods themselves, it was a pharaoh's duty to represent their people to the gods and to satisfy the gods.

Words to Know

absolute power: complete control over a government and/or organized group of people.

Horus: a falcon god and the son of Osiris, the head of the underworld.

underworld: the world of the dead.

crook: (*heka scepter*) an item often carried by kings and considered a symbol for "rule" or "ruler." It looked like a short cane or shepherd's staff.

flail: (*nekhakha*) an item often carried by kings, along with their crook, as a symbol of power. It looked like a short rod with three beaded strands attached.

Hatshepsut: the first known woman to be an ancient Egyptian pharaoh. She ruled from about 1473 to 1458 BCE.

Cleopatra: a Greek queen and pharaoh who ruled Egypt from around 51 to 30 BCE. She was the last pharaoh.

Royal crook and flail.

Then the gods would keep the Nile flooding to ensure bountiful harvests. It is even believed that kings were responsible for making sure the sun rose every morning! In general, they were in charge of keeping order, truth, and justice in balance. This balance was a concept called ma'at. If a king failed at maintaining ma'at, he (or she) was blamed entirely.

In art, kings and gods are frequently shown holding two items in the shape of an X across their chests. One item is a **crook** (or *heka scepter*), which has long been a symbol for "rule" or "ruler" and is like a short cane or shepherds' staff. And the other item is a

Famous Women Rulers

According to the list of kings, there were not many ancient Egyptian rulers who were women. There were, however, at least four. Two of the most famous female rulers also happen to be the first and last ones we know about it: **Hatshepsut** and **Cleopatra**.

Hatshepsut was the daughter of Thutmose I and Queen Ahmose and was married to her half brother. (Marrying within your family was common among royalty as they wished to carry on the family line.) Her husband had a son from another wife. When Thutmose and the other men in line for the throne died, Hatshepsut's stepson took over. Because he was too young to rule, Hatshepsut ruled along with him. This practice is called co-regency. Eventually, Hatshepsut decided she wanted to be the only ruler and so she declared herself king. To get around the fact that kings were supposed to be *sons* of gods, Hatshepsut told the people of Egypt that the god Amun-Ra spoke to her. She also dressed like a man and wore the common false beard of kings. Hatshepsut ruled Egypt very successfully from about 1473 to 1458 BCE. She disappeared in 1458 BCE, around the same time Thutmose III led a revolt to take over the throne.

Hatshepsut

flail (or *nekhakha*), which is a short rod that has three beaded strands attached. It resembles a modern-day harvesting tool called a *ladanisterion,* and may have been used in ancient times for farming. Some Egyptologists believe the flail might have represented the fertility of the land in ancient times. Kings carried a crook and flail during ceremonies and were even mummified with their hands across their chests so they could hold them in the afterlife. For some unknown reason, one of ancient Egypt's most famous kings, King Tut, was buried without his crook and flail. Instead, several were found separately and in different parts of the tomb.

In addition to the crook and flail, kings also wore special crowns. They were not like the gold, pointy ones we often think of from

Cleopatra was a Greek queen who ruled Egypt from around 51 to 30 BCE. She was a member of the Ptolemy family, the Greeks who ruled Egypt after Alexander the Great conquered Egypt. She was the last pharaoh—male or female—to rule what we consider *ancient* Egypt. She was around 17 when she took over the throne, and, like Hatshepsut, was a savvy and skilled leader. She was said to be very charming and smart—she even spoke nine languages!

As was required by law, Cleopatra shared the rule with her brother, who was also her husband. After her brother and first husband, Ptolemy XIII died, Cleopatra married her younger half-brother Ptolemy XIV. Through both of Cleopatra's marriages, she was really the one in charge of the throne. In 48 BCE, she met the Roman leader Julius Caesar. She later gave birth to his son. After Caesar was murdered in 44 BCE, two Roman leaders, Marc Antony and Octavian, battled for control of the Roman Empire.

Meanwhile, Cleopatra became romantically involved with Marc Antony. In 32 BCE, Rome declared war on Egypt and there was a great battle off the coast of Greece. Octavian won and Antony and Cleopatra returned to Egypt. There, Antony killed himself. Heartbroken, Cleopatra committed suicide shortly afterward in 30 BCE. Legend has it she killed herself with an asp, a poisonous snake.

Cleopatra

Red crown of Lower Egypt.

fairy tales. They were colorful crowns, rather, that were more like tall, fancy hats. There were many different styles and colors of crowns—three of which are familiar to us today. The first is the **red crown** (or *deshret*). This crown was worn by the king of Lower Egypt and, from the side, looks kind of like a chair with a pointy, slanted back. The king of Upper Egypt wore the **white crown** (or *hedjet*). It looks kind of like a bowling pin with a fat bottom. After Lower and Upper Egypt were united, one person ruled the land. The kings who ruled after unification wore the **double crown**

White crown of Upper Egypt.

Famous Pharaohs

Khufu (also known as Cheops)—Khufu ruled from 2589 to 2566 BCE. There is not much known about him as a ruler, though some texts suggest he was not well-loved. His main claim to fame is that he built the Great Pyramid at Giza. This pyramid, near modern-day Cairo, is the largest pyramid in the world. Although part of it is now missing, it once stood 481 feet tall and took up about 13 acres. It is the only surviving wonder of the original Seven Wonders of the Ancient World. The Great Pyramid draws 5,000 visitors a day!

Akhenaton (also known as Amenhotop IV)—Akhenaton ruled from 1352 to 1336 BCE. He was married to the famously beautiful Queen Nefertiti and is thought to be the father of Tutankhamen. (Tutankhamen's mother was most likely not Queen Nefertiti but one of Akhenaton's other wives.) Akhenaton is often called the "heretic king." This is because during his rule he called for religious reform that caused a great stir in ancient Egypt. Up until his reign, Egyptians believed in and worshipped many gods. Akhenaton declared that there was only one god, or a head god, called Aton.

King Tutankhamen (also know as King Tut)—King Tut ruled from 1336 to 1327 BCE. He was crowned at age nine and was therefore known as the "boy king." He ruled only for a very short time,

Akhenaton

Did You Know?

In order to keep kings' tombs safe from tomb robbers, people in the New Kingdom (1550–1069 BCE) buried kings in a secret place. This secret place was a remote valley west of Thebes. It is now called the Valley of the Kings. Tombs in this valley are mostly long tunnels that lead to burial chambers. Because of all the digging necessary, one of the first jobs of a new king was to choose his burial site so work on the tomb could begin! There is a Valley of the Queens, too. It is located south of the Valley of the Kings.

Double crown of unified Egypt.

around 10 years, and probably would have been forgotten altogether by history if it hadn't been for his famous tomb. Why is his tomb so famous? There are two main reasons. First, King Tut's tomb, which is in the Valley of the Kings, was found much later than most other tombs, unearthed in 1922 by Howard Carter and Lord Carnarvon. Secondly, it is the only one found intact in modern times. This means that despite being robbed in ancient days (evidence suggest at least two break-ins), it was resealed and left untouched for thousands of years! The riches inside the small tomb were so precious and plentiful that it took 10 years to properly remove them all. Many of the artifacts have traveled the world in an exhibit. King Tut's mummy was once on display as well. Today, though, it rests in the Valley of the Kings—the only king to remain buried there.

Rameses II (also know as Rameses the Great)—Rameses II ruled from 1279 to 1213 BCE. He took the throne at around age 20 and ruled until he was a very old man. (It is said he lived to be 99 years old.) He was responsible for more monuments and temples than any other king. He was also a renowned soldier who signed the world's first-known peace treaty with his enemies. Rameses' tomb was found empty but his mummy has been recovered. In fact, Rameses' mummy is considered to be one of the most well-preserved mummies ever to be found.

Rameses II

The uraeus.

(or *pschent*). It was a combination of the white and red crowns. The striking cobra you see on crowns is called a **uraeus**. It represented the "eye of Ra" and was there to show the king's power and wisdom in overseeing everything.

Because records and dates were not always kept or because ancient Egyptians didn't record dates in the same way we do, there's no way to be sure if we know about all the ancient rulers or when they ruled. Around 300 BCE, though, an Egyptian priest and scholar named Manetho set out to chronicle the history of the kings of ancient Egypt and created a list of 170 kings that ruled Egypt over time.

Words to Know

red crown: (*deshret*) the crown worn by the king of Lower Egypt.

white crown: (*hedjet*) the crown that the king of Upper Egypt wore.

double crown: (*pschent*) the crown worn by ancient Egyptian kings after Upper and Lower Egypt were united. It is a combination of the white and red crowns.

uraeus: the cobra featured on the double crown that represents the eye of Ra, the sun god.

Make Your Own Crook

1 Straighten the coat hanger and carefully cut a 12-inch piece. It's okay if the wire is slightly bent, but the next step will be easier if it's straight.

2 Fold a section of newspaper in half and tear it at the fold so that you have two pieces of newspaper that are about 12 inches wide. Lay your wire on the paper and begin rolling it up. Make sure to keep the roll as tight as you can. The wire will be inside the roll. When you're done, use a small piece of tape to keep the roll from unraveling.

3 Insert about 3 inches of your rolled up newspaper/wire into the pipe. It should fit pretty snugly, but if it doesn't, use a piece of tape to keep it in place. If it's too big to fit into the pipe, you can pinch or fold the bottom to make it fit.

4 Use the white duct tape to cover the newspaper/wire. Make sure you use a small piece to cover the end, or tip. Next, bend the newspaper/wire to resemble the top of a king's crook.

5 Once you have the shape of a crook, you can cover the rest of the handle with duct tape, if you want. Doing so will give your crook a uniform look. Decorate your crook with permanent markers. You can also spray paint the crook any color you want, following the directions on the paint can. One of King Tut's crooks had blue and gold stripes. Experiment with some fancy designs of your own!

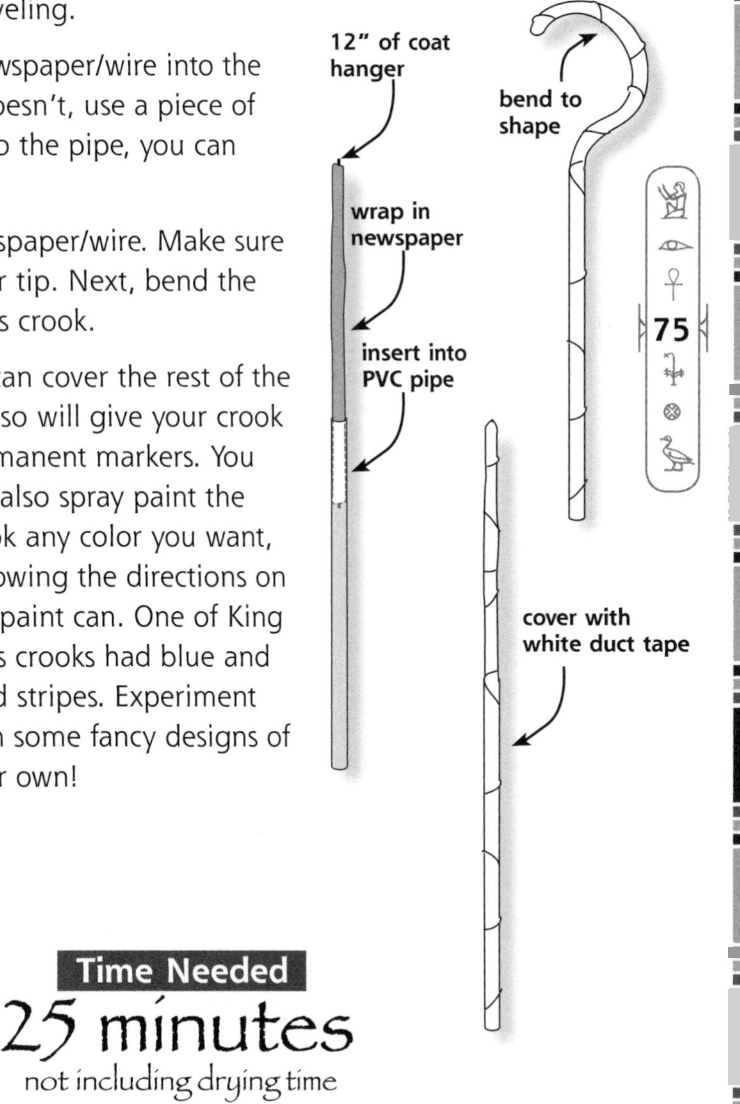

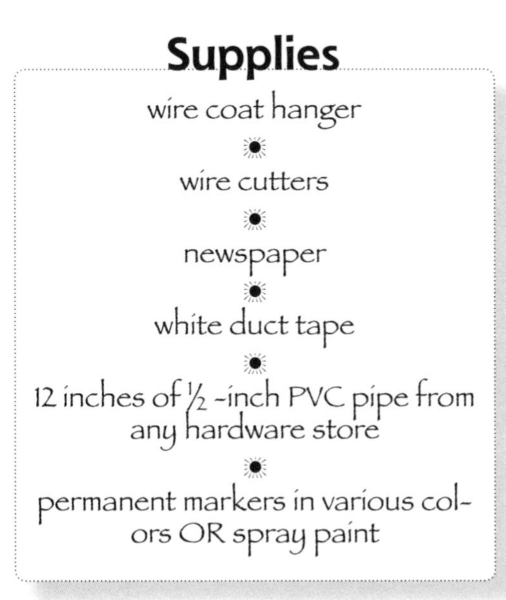

Supplies

wire coat hanger

wire cutters

newspaper

white duct tape

12 inches of ½-inch PVC pipe from any hardware store

permanent markers in various colors OR spray paint

Time Needed

25 minutes

not including drying time

Make Your Own Flail

1 Thread each piece of yarn through one of the small pieces of drinking straw. Tie the straw to the bottom of the yarn with a knot. This will keep the other straw pieces from sliding off the end of the yarn. Tip: it's easier to thread the yarn through the straw if you put a small piece of tape around the tip of the yarn.

2 Thread various pieces of the straws onto the yarn. You can make a pattern or a random design. Leave about 3 inches of yarn at the top of each piece. When you're done with all three, tie the pieces of yarn together.

tie pieces of yarn together

3 Push the knot and any extra yarn into the plastic pipe. Use a small piece of tape to secure the beaded strands to the pipe.

4 Next, decorate the handle of your flail with permanent markers or spray paint. (You can cover the handle with white duct tape first if you want to make your crook and flail a matching set.) Now walk around, looking and feeling just like an Egyptian king!

pieces of drinking straws

stuff yarn knot into pipe

Variation: The beads on flails tended to be long. That is why these directions use plastic straws. But instead of straw pieces, you can use plastic beads. And instead of yarn, you can use thin leather cord. You can find both of these things at any craft store. They are usually kept with the jewelry-making supplies.

Supplies

- 5 or 6 brightly colored drinking straws cut into various lengths (make sure to have 3 small pieces, each about a half an inch long)
- 3 pieces of yarn, cut into 15-inch lengths
- 15 inches of ½-inch PVC pipe from any hardware store
- white duct tape
- permanent markers

Time Needed

20 minutes

not including drying time

Make Your Own Throne

In ancient Egypt, chairs with armrests were reserved for important or powerful people, like royalty. The legs of chairs were shorter than those on our chairs, and the legs were often carved to look like the legs of animals. If you have an old chair, you can make your own royal throne.

1 With the help of an adult, saw 3 to 6 inches off of each chair leg. (How much you cut depends on how short you want the throne to be, or how much you can cut off the chair leg without making it unsafe.)

2 If the chair has a padded seat, remove the seat. Next, paint the throne gold. You can put the seat back on once the paint is dry.

3 When the paint is dry, use whatever decorations you'd like to jazz up the throne. Sometimes, chairs were decorated with pictures of gods. You can add a drawing of your favorite ancient Egyptian god, too. Now, you're ready to sit like a king!

Supplies

an old, wooden chair with or without armrests (you can often find inexpensive ones at garage sales)

saw (ask an adult to help with this!)

gold paint or gold spray paint

decorations such as glitter, sequins, fancy buttons, trim, and permanent markers

several pieces of thick cardboard OR air-hardening clay

Variation: You can add animal legs to your throne. Sketch out the animal legs you'd like on the cardboard. Cut them out and attach to the chair legs with tape or glue *before* painting. You can also sculpt animal legs around the chair legs with air-hardening clay. Let the clay dry completely before painting. This may take several days.

13 Pyramids

There is, perhaps, nothing in the world quite as enduring and mystical as the ancient pyramids. Built thousands of years ago, about 100 of these huge and impressive feats of engineering are still standing in modern Egypt. But why were the pyramids built? And how did the ancient Egyptians build them?

Pyramids are monuments that house the tombs of pharaohs, and all the things he or she needed in the afterlife. Before pyramids, kings were buried in brick tombs called **mastabas**. These weren't very grand, and tomb robbers could break into them easily. During the Old Kingdom, the ancient Egyptians began experimenting with new designs. Around 2750 BCE, the first pyramid was built. It was designed for King Djoser by Imhotep, a famous doctor, writer, and archi-

Did You Know?

The Egyptian word for pyramid was *mer*, which means "place of ascension."

Step Pyramid of Saqqara.

tect. King Djoser's pyramid is known as the Step Pyramid of Saqqara. Step pyramids look the way they sound—like steps. King Djoser's pyramid has six steps. It also has a rectangular base like a mastaba tomb. It is about 200 feet tall, and the burial chamber is underground.

After King Djoser's step pyramid came King Snefru's Pyramid at Meidum. This pyramid is a step pyramid too. It was the first pyramid to have a burial chamber that was above ground. It had eight steps, and several of the bottom steps were filled in to make smooth sides. Today, only the top three steps are visible, and the slopes are all gone. Some experts believe they collapsed, while others suggest the stones were taken for other projects.

Words to Know

mastaba: rectangular, brick tombs.

sarcophagus: a large stone box where coffins were placed.

pyramid text: sacred writing on the inner walls of pyramids.

sledge: a simple machine that uses logs and a platform to move heavy objects.

primeval mound: a sacred and mythical mound where the ancient Egyptians believed the sun first rose and life was created.

King Snefru also built the Bent Pyramid at Dahshur. It is believed that this odd-looking pyramid was the first attempt at what we call a true pyramid. (A true pyramid is a perfect pyramid, one that has a square base and four equal triangular sides that meet at a point at the top.) This pyramid is unique for two reasons. For one, it had two entrances. Secondly, and more importantly, its sides change angles about two-thirds of the way up. This change in angle gives it its odd "bent" shape, so that it looks kind of like a pyramid with rounded sides. We don't know for sure why the

Did You Know?

People who could not afford fancy tombs were buried in cemeteries. Sacred animals such as birds and baboons were also buried in cemeteries.

The Bent Pyramid at Dahshur.

Bent Pyramid is shaped the way it is. Evidence shows the design was altered mid-construction. Many Egyptologists believe this was done for safety reasons; the builders most likely realized the structure would be unsafe if they continued to build at the original angle. Other Egyptologists believe the collapsed walls of the Pyramid at Meidum are what made the builders change their plans.

King Snefru built one other pyramid, and this one is considered the first true pyramid. (Apparently the third time really is the charm!) This pyramid is known as the Red Pyramid due to the reddish limestone that was used to build its core and is now exposed. However, it is also known as the North Pyramid or the Shining Pyramid. It has a large base and a gentle slope, so it spreads out more than some other pyramids. King Snefru may have been buried in the Red Pyramid at one time, although we don't really know for sure. A **sarcophagus** and skeleton found in a mastaba nearby might have been the king's remains, but before they could be studied, they mysteriously disappeared.

A sarcophagus.

About 150 years after the first step pyramid was built, King Khufu commissioned the granddaddy of all the pyramids—the Great Pyramid of Giza. Originally 481 feet tall, with a base that was 754 feet long on each side, the Great Pyramid is the tallest pyramid in the world. Due to the wear and tear of time, and because people have taken stone from it, however, the pyramid is now 449 feet tall, and the sides are 745 feet long. This pyramid is made up of

Did You Know?

King Khafra, son of King Khufu, wanted his pyramid to be bigger than his dad's. While it's not taller, it looks like it might be because it is built on higher ground.

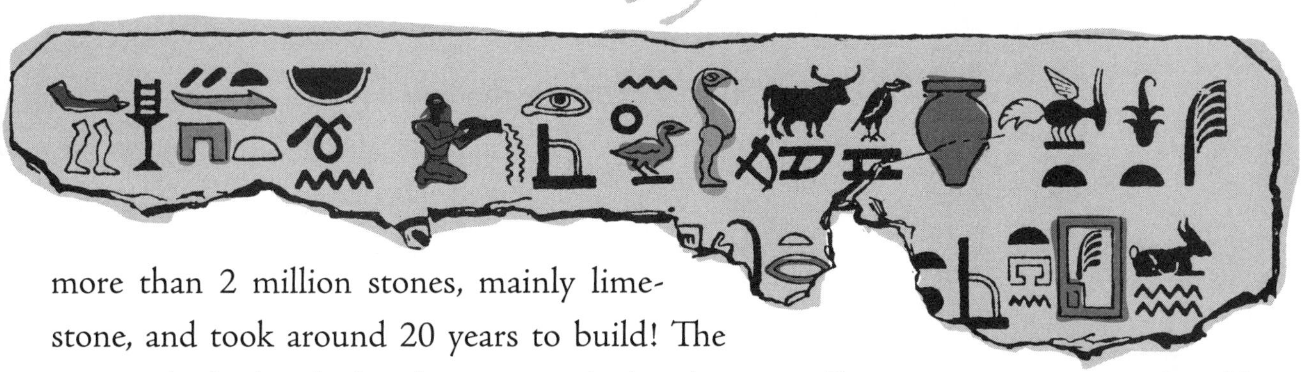

more than 2 million stones, mainly limestone, and took around 20 years to build! The interior had a king's chamber, a queen's chamber, as well as an unfinished, underground chamber. Unlike other pyramid chambers, which are covered in sacred writing called **pyramid text**, King Khufu's burial chamber walls are mysteriously bare. Near the Great Pyramid are three other, smaller pyramids and mastabas where King Khufu's relatives and officials were buried.

Pyramid text.

As is common with many Egyptian pyramids, the Great Pyramid is surrounded by what is called a pyramid complex. Temples, mortuary temples (places where funerals were carried out and food offerings were left), and walkways to get from building to building were in these complexes. The priests who worked at the pyramid temples lived nearby.

In the 1950s, an amazing discovery was made near Khufu's Great Pyramid: a pit was found, and inside the pit was a dismantled boat. This large boat, often called the Solar Boat or the Royal Ship of Khufu, was reassembled. Boats like this one were long and skinny with turned-up ends in which the ancient Egyptians believed the sun god, Ra, traveled. Today, this reconstructed boat can be seen inside a special museum built right above the pit.

Even though we know why the pyramids were built, we are not certain just *how* the ancient Egyptians built them. It's generally accepted that stones were quarried nearby using simple tools, such as

A representation of the Solar Boat carrying the pharaoh to the underworld.

chisels, or other stone and copper tools. Another tool they used to cut stones was water. Yes—water! The ancient Egyptians would chisel a hole into stone, slip a piece of dry wood into the hole, and then wet the wood. As the wood absorbed the water it would expand and break up the stone.

After the stones were cut, they had to be moved. Stones were transported by river barge, when necessary, and then moved over the desert sand with rope and a **sledge**. A sledge is a simple machine that uses logs and a platform to roll objects. The Egyptians may have also moved sleds carrying the stones over ground that had been wetted down.

Stonecutters at work.

Did You Know?

Stones used to make pyramids include limestone, sandstone, and granite.

Once they were at the building site, the stones had to be put into place. Because we've never found any blueprints or instructions, we don't know how the ancient Egyptians lifted the stones into place. The ancient Egyptians didn't have cranes, like we do, or even pulleys. Most experts believe the pyramid builders must have used ramps and levers of some sort, although no evidence of this has been found. Ramps may have been built alongside the pyramids or (less likely) spiraled around them.

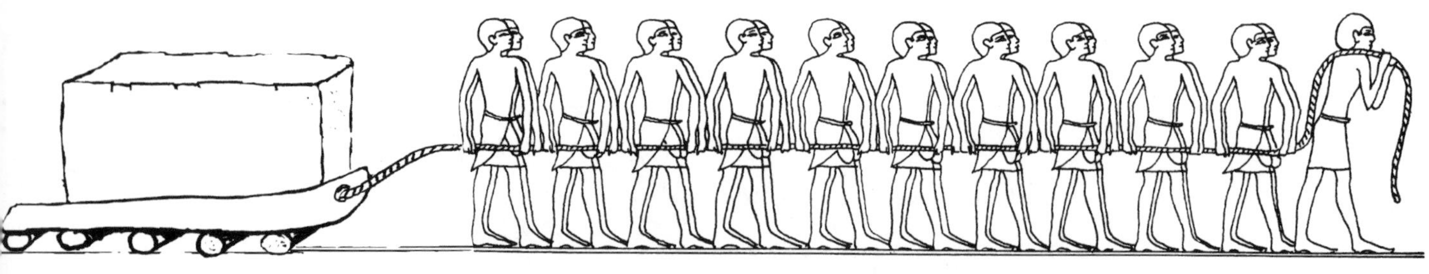

Workers using a sledge to move a giant block.

It's possible, too, that the ancient Egyptians had some other tool or system that we just don't know about.

Did You Know?

There are no interior doors inside pyramids. The ancient Egyptians didn't believe they were necessary; kings who were dead could come and go as they pleased.

Who built the pyramids? Because of the imagination of ancient writers and, more recently, Hollywood movie producers, myth has it that slaves built the pyramids. *This isn't true!* While *some* slaves were likely used, there was probably a group of skilled workers who worked on building all year round. Builders may have come from the area or been recruited from other regions. During the flooding season, when farmers were unable to work their land, it's likely that they too joined in on the construction. Building a pyramid may have been seen as respectable work—a way to honor the king or serve the community. In recent years, writing inside the Great Pyramid of Giza walls left by work crews, who called themselves "Friends of Khufu," suggests that builders worked happily and willingly.

In the past, it's been said that it took 100,000 workers to build a pyramid. Modern Egyptologists believe the number is actually between 20,000 and 30,000. Recent excavations have turned up evidence that workers lived in camps or villages near the building site. These camps were well organized and provided necessary food and shelter for all the workers. For example, evidence of bakeries, breweries, butcher shops, and cemeteries has been found.

There's one more mystery about pyramids: no one knows why ancient Egyptians chose the pyramid shape itself. Maybe they were built that way so the kings could "step" into heaven, or maybe they were supposed to represent some kind of boat in which a king could sail into

Did You Know?

The Great Pyramids are not only the oldest of the Seven Wonders of the Ancient World. They are also the only wonder still in existence today.

Did You Know?

Because pyramids have withstood the test of time, the Middle East has a saying: "Time fears no man, yet time fears the pyramids."

the afterlife. Some experts believe ancient Egyptians built the pyramids to look like the **primeval mound**, a sacred and mythical mound where the ancient Egyptians believed the sun first rose and life was created.

The Pharos: The Oldest Known Lighthouse

Have you ever heard of the Seven Wonders of the Ancient World? It was a list, made by the Greeks during the second century BCE, of the seven most important architectural feats built between 2700 and 270 BCE. The Great Pyramid of Giza was on this list. Another of the great wonders was the **Pharos**, or Lighthouse of Alexandria. The world's oldest known lighthouse, the Pharos was built near the harbor of Alexandria, Egypt, and safely guided sailors for 1500 years. It was so well known that *pharos* eventually came to mean "lighthouse" in several languages.

Work on the lighthouse began in 290 BCE. Like most structures built in ancient Egypt, it took a long time to complete—around 20 years. Although this ancient marvel was destroyed (most likely by earthquakes) around 1325 CE, we know about it because travelers left detailed descriptions of it. The Pharos didn't look like the tall, cylinder-shaped tower lighthouses we have today. It looked more like a box or mini skyscraper. It was about 400 feet high, which made it the second-tallest structure in the world at the time. The Great Pyramid of Giza was taller. A mirror, possibly made with a piece of polished copper, was used to direct a fire's light at night or the sun's light during the day.

The Lighthouse of Alexandria.

There's an interesting tale about the lighthouse's designer, Sostrates of Knidos. As the story goes, Sostrates was proud of his work and wanted to put his name on it. The problem was that Ptolemy II, the ruler at the time, wanted *his* name on the lighthouse, too. What did Sostrates do? He put the inscription he wanted, the one with his own name, on the foundation, and then he covered it with plaster inscribed with Ptolemy's name. In time, the plaster wore off and the original inscription remained!

Make Your Own Pyramid

The Great Pyramid of Giza is the biggest pyramid ever built. To get an idea of just how enormous this ancient wonder is, here are instructions for building a model that is approximately 1,000 times smaller. When you're done try to imagine what your pyramid would look like if it was 1,000 times bigger.

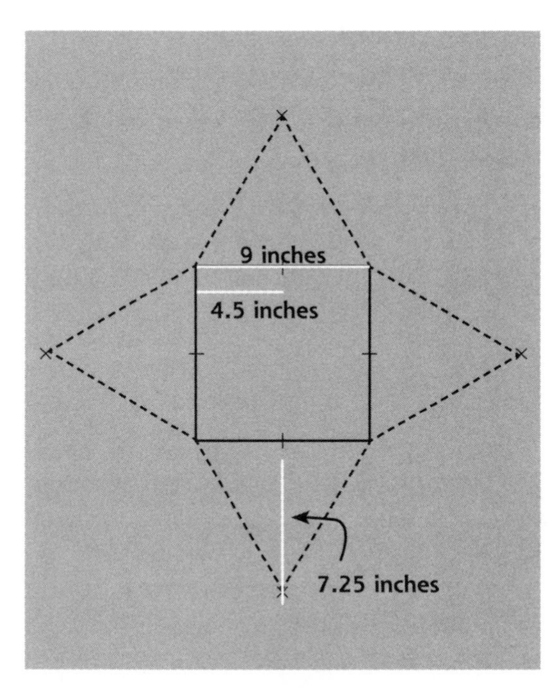

1 Use your ruler and pencil to mark a square that is 9 inches by 9 inches in the center of your poster board.

2 Use your ruler to find the middle of each side of the square (this will be at 4.5 inches). Make a mark at this point.

3 From each of the center marks, measure out from the square 7.25 inches. Make a small x with your pencil. Draw a line from the x to the two nearest corners of the square. When you're done, you should have a square surrounded by four triangles, equal in size. Cut the entire figure out.

4 If you want to paint or decorate your pyramid, turn it over to the side you didn't draw the lines on. Only the triangles will show once you've assembled your pyramid. When you're ready, turn it over again and carefully fold the triangles up to form the pyramid shape. Secure the sides with tape. (You can decorate it after you put it together, but it's a little harder to do.)

5 Ta-da! You've just built a pyramid! Some people believe the pyramid shape has special powers. This is probably just superstition, of course, but if you want to try out the theory, tape a piece of string to the top of your pyramid, hang your pyramid over your desk or your bed, and see what happens.

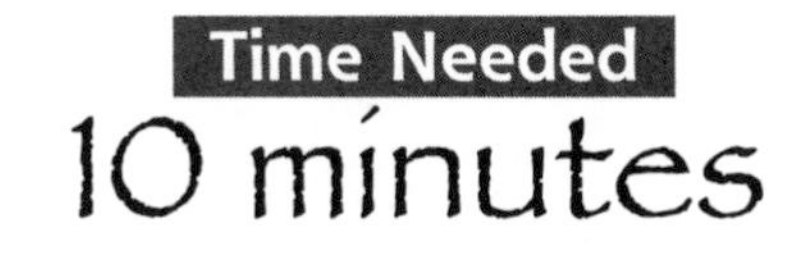

Make Your Own Sledge

1 Lay the five branch pieces on the ground, an equal distance apart and parallel to each other. How far apart you place them depends on how long your platform is.

2 Carefully lay your square piece of wood or cardboard on top of these "rollers." Now you have a sledge! Don't worry if the sledge platform is wider than the rollers or if the rollers are longer than the platform—your sledge will still work.

3 Next, put whatever you'd like to move on top of your sledge. Move the object by gently pushing on the platform. Eventually, the platform will roll off the end roller. When this happens, simply pick up the last roller and place it under the front of the platform. Repeat this process until your object is where you want it to be. Now, you're rolling along just like the pyramid builders! Can you see how a sledge helped them transport huge stones?

Supplies

a long, straight tree branch that is smooth, cut into five equal lengths OR cut up a wooden dowel or an old broomstick

a flat rectangular or square piece of wood, OR a piece of corrugated cardboard, for your sledge platform

an object you'd like to move, like a toy, a book, a pair of shoes, or a block—use your imagination!

Time Needed

15 minutes

Did You Know?

To measure length, ancient Egyptians used a wood or granite rod called a royal cubit. (These were kind of like the wooden or plastic rulers we use today.) A royal cubit was the approximate length of a man's forearm and hand, or about 20 inches.

1 Royal Cubit

14 Temples

The ancient Egyptians believed that their gods could inhabit statues, and they believed that these statues needed a place to "live." So Egyptians built temples. The Egyptian word for temple meant "God's house." In early history, temples were small, simple buildings, but later temples were huge, elaborate stone buildings that were often surrounded by beautiful gardens and magnificent statues.

Although they were built with stone, not all of the ancient Egyptian temples are still around; they've fallen down, or were torn down or destroyed by thieves. Other buildings were built over the temple sites. The temple remains that are left, though, can help give us an idea of just how big many of the temples were and how they were designed and used. One of the best-preserved examples is the Karnak Temple, which isn't really one temple but a huge complex of religious structures. The building of the Karnak began in the Middle

Statue of Rameses II among the ruins of the Karnak Temple.

Kingdom, and it was added onto by many rulers for the next 2,000 years! (Most of the buildings are dedicated to the god **Amun**.) The complex covers over 240 acres and even has a rectangular, man-made, sacred lake that is 393 feet by 252 feet, or about the size of an adult soccer field.

Nearby is another temple complex called the Luxor Temple. Like the temples at Karnak, the buildings at Luxor were added onto over the years by different rulers. What's neat about these two places is that they're connected by a road lined with sphinxes and ram heads!

We usually think of temples as being churches, but temples in ancient Egypt were not used the way churches are. Ancient Egyptian temples were more like meeting places than places where people prayed. Though common folk could wander the temple grounds, they were not allowed inside the shrines of the temples, where the statues of a god were kept. Only priests and pharaohs

Did You Know?

The pharaoh was considered the supreme high priest. Because he could not usually be at the temple every day, a picture or statue of the pharaoh tending to the needs of the gods was kept inside the sacred shrine.

Ruins of the Temple at Luxor.

Who is the Sun God, Amun or Ra?

Before Amun became a god, the word "amun" started out simply as the concept of air. As time passed, this concept grew in importance to become the breath of life. Amun was depicted as a man and considered a god. More time passed and Amun's importance grew until he became the father of the gods and the sun god. At this time, Amun and Ra (who was previously the creator and sun god) merged identities and names, becoming one god, Amun-Ra.

Amun

were allowed in the shrines. If someone wanted to make an offering of food or other goods, they left these items by a fake, recessed doorway where the god could accept gifts. Some of the false doors even had small trenches that allowed wine to flow to the god.

Just what did the ancient Egyptian temples look like? They were magnificent in size and beauty! There was no single design, but most of them had huge gateways called pylons. Beyond the pylons were hypostyle halls, which are chambers where columns or pillars hold up the ceilings. They kind of look like forests made of stones! In the Great Hypostyle Hall at Karnak, some of the 134 columns are nearly 70 feet tall. The hall is so large that it could hold the Notre Dame Cathedral. Beyond the hall was the sanctuary, the holiest part of the temple, and inside the sanctuary was the shrine where the actual statue was kept. Temples typically had courtyards and a room for offerings and were surrounded by an enclosure wall.

Temple complexes were more than just places that housed one of the gods. They were like mini towns with offices, stores, workshops, libraries, and places where scribes and priests were trained. The priests and their families lived in

Words to Know

Amun: in Egyptian mythology, the supreme god and the god of the sun.

bark shrine: where the statue of a god was kept when it was carried through the streets on festival days.

Isis: the ancient Egyptian goddess of motherhood. She was Osiris's wife and Horus's mother.

obelisk: monuments with a pointed top that the ancient Egyptians often placed next to temples or tombs.

Priests carrying a bark shrine.

nearby houses. Local government offices were near the temple, and "court" was often held in the temple courtyards. This was so the gods could watch and make sure justice was done.

During festivals the ancient Egyptians got as close as they ever did to the statues of any god; ancient Egyptians would line the streets and watch as these divine statues were carried past them. During the festival of Opet, for example, the statues of Amun and other gods were moved from Karnak to Luxor. During the Valley Festival (also called the Beautiful Feast of the Valley), statues of Amun, Mut (his wife), and Khons (his son) were moved from Karnak to Deir el-Bahri, a funeral site west of the Nile.

Although the Egyptians were close to these statues during festivals, they never actually saw them. The statues of gods were carried inside a **bark shrine**—a special carrier, often shaped like a boat, that housed the *naos* (or box) where the statue was kept. These barks are often seen in pictures being carried on long poles.

Sometimes during festivals, people would ask a god a question or

Did You Know?

Sometimes ancient Egyptian temples and statues were built to honor the living pharaohs. King Rameses II, for instance, had numerous, large statues made in his likeness, as well as a temple built. Rameses' temple, in Abu Simbel, was built in such a way that twice a year the rising sun lights up the sanctuary and the statues at the back of the temple.

Popular Gods

The ancient Egyptians worshipped hundreds of gods. There were two main types of gods: principal (or state) gods and household gods.

Principal gods were worshipped by most ancient Egyptians. The two most familiar were Ra (the sun god, later known as Amun-Ra) and Osiris (god of the underworld). Other principal gods included Anubis (the jackal-headed god who looked after the dead and oversaw mummification), **Isis** (Osiris's wife), Ma'at (Osiris's daughter), Hapy (the god of the Nile), and Horus (a falcon god and son of Osiris). These powerful gods had temples and special statues built in their honor.

Isis

Different household gods were worshipped in different parts of ancient Egypt. They usually didn't have big followings and therefore didn't have big, state temples. Two of the most familiar household gods were Bes (the dwarf-like god of children and fun and games) and Taweret (the hippo-like god who protected mothers and children).

for advice about a problem. Since the god statue couldn't reply, a priest would answer for him. This was one of the many jobs of a priest. Ancient Egyptian priests were not really religious leaders; they did not preach. They were men who were in charge of taking care of the statues and temples. (The Egyptian word for priest, *hem netjer,* meant "servant of god.") Priests, who were appointed by the pharaoh or inherited the position from family members, were responsible for running the temples. Every day, the high priest opened the shrine, washed and dressed the statue, and left food for the god. Other priests took care of the temple and the temple grounds. This meant cleaning, gardening, and

A priest burning incense at the festival of the Nile's flooding.

taking care of all business issues, like taxes, for example. Because the temples were so big and so many people visited them, priests often worked in shifts, usually lasting for a month at a time. When priests were on duty, they had to follow strict rules, including shaving their head, bathing several times a day, and wearing certain clothes.

A priest preparing onions for an offering.

Obelisks

Obelisks are tall, skinny, solid stone monuments with pointed tops that resemble a pyramid. They are found all over the world. For example, though not a real obelisk because it is not solid stone, the Washington Monument is obelisk-shaped.

In ancient Egypt, obelisks had to do with the sun or the worship of the sun. Some believe they might have been shaped to look like the sun's rays. Small obelisks were sometimes placed outside of tombs. During the New Kingdom, obelisks were placed in pairs by the temple pylons. Today, unfortunately, there are no obelisk pairs standing together in their original locations. Obelisks were also sometimes erected to celebrate an anniversary or war victory.

Every year, thousands of tourists visit an obelisk that lies in a quarry in Aswan. This obelisk was damaged while it was being cut out of the granite. Had it been completed and erected, it would have measured about 137 feet tall and weighed almost as much as a dozen cars! The tallest obelisk in the world today is 107 feet and is located in Rome, Italy.

Make Your Own Obelisk

cut in half to make a square length of foam

A drawing of the obelisk known as Cleopatra's needle.

This project requires a sharp knife so make sure you have an adult to help.

1 Cover your workspace with newspapers. You need the florist foam to have square ends so cut it accordingly. Most florist foam comes in rectangular blocks. The easiest way to make a square-based piece of foam is to lay the foam down and cut it in half, lengthwise.

2 Obelisks have pyramid-shaped tops, so carefully use the knife to carve one end into a pyramid. You can practice on a piece of scrap foam to figure out the best carving technique.

Supplies

newspapers

12-inch-long block of florist foam (from the floral arrangement aisle of any craft store)

glue

a sharp knife

4-by-4-inch wood base (from the woodworking section of a craft store)

small can of sand- or stone-colored spray paint

3 Use the tip of the knife to carve hieroglyphs into the long sides of your obelisk. You can also use a pen or a toothpick to carve the symbols.

4 Stand the obelisk up (the pyramid should be at the top) and glue it to the wooden base. Let the glue dry for a few minutes.

5 Spray paint the foam obelisk according to the directions on the spray paint can. Because the foam will absorb some of the paint, you may need a couple of coats.

Variation: If you can't find florist foam, Styrofoam will work, too. It's not as easy to carve as the florist foam, though.

Make Your Own Peek-Inside Sanctuary

1 Paint the outside of your shoebox white. When the paint is dry, use the other paints or markers to decorate the outside. Evidence shows that Egyptian temples were brightly painted and sometimes even had precious jewels embedded into them.

2 The easiest way to decorate the inside of your shoebox is to make designs on drawing paper, then glue the paper to the inside of the box. You can do this for the outside too. To make sure the paper will fit properly, trace each side of the box onto the drawing paper. Draw pictures on the paper before cutting out the pieces and gluing them to the "walls" and "floor" of your sanctuary. You can decorate the "ceiling" too (the inside of the shoebox lid), but you will be poking holes in it later, so keep this mind.

Supplies

- 1 shoebox, with lid
- white, water-based paint
- colored pencils, markers, paint, other decorations
- drawing paper
- pencil
- scissors
- glue
- 1 small jewelry box (this box doesn't need a lid) OR the bottom of a pint-size milk carton that's been washed and dried
- masking tape
- modeling clay

3 Turn the jewelry box or milk carton so it's lying on one side. Tape it to the bottom of your shoebox, near one of the ends. This will be your shrine. You can paint your shrine gold or decorate it in some other way, too, if you'd like.

Time Needed
25 minutes
not including drying time

4 Using modeling clay, sculpt a small statue of a god and put it inside your shrine. You can use the clay to make other things to offer the god as well. For example, make a plate of food or a vase with flowers and place them near your shrine. If you have any scrap pieces of fabric, you can even make clothes for your statue. Be sure to glue or tape your items to the box so they don't roll around when you pick up the box.

5 When the inside is complete, put the lid on the shoebox. Carefully poke 5 to 10 holes all around the lid. The holes don't have to be very big; they just have to let in a little bit of light. You can use pointy scissors or the point of a pen. You might want to ask an adult for help with this if the lid is thick.

6 At the end of the box opposite your shrine, carefully cut a hole about the size of a quarter. This is your viewing hole.

7 Now, hold your sanctuary up to the light and peek inside. You'll be able to see the shrine and your wall drawings.

holes for light

hole for viewing

Did You Know?

Sometimes ancient Egyptian builders would dig special pits near temples, tombs, and pyramids, and they put models of tools, food, and other things inside. These "buried treasures" are called foundation deposits. Ancient Egyptians believed the deposits would convince the gods to protect the buildings.

15 Mummies

Pyramids, temples, elaborate tombs, funeral boats, and mummies: these things might make it seem as if the ancient Egyptians thought about death all the time. However it wasn't death they were focused on, but life *after* death. And mummies demonstrate this fascination in an interesting (and creepy!) way.

Ancient Egyptians believed a person was made of many parts: the Physical Body, the Name, the **Ba**, the **Ka**, the **Akh**, and the **Shadow**. The Body and the Name are easy to understand. Like many cultures, ancient Egyptians believed a person's name had magical and protective power. But the Ba, Ka, and Akh are more difficult concepts to grasp. From studying texts and tombs, Egyptologists know that the Ba was what we might call a person's personality. The Ka was a spiritual twin that followed a person around unseen throughout his or her life. And the Akh was what was formed when the Ba and Ka reunited after death. The Shadow was the protector of all these parts. Ancient Egyptians also believed that in order to live on forever, a person needed his or her body in the afterlife. In order to preserve the body, ancient Egyptians mummified their dead.

A mummy, a coffin, and a sarcophagus.

Strangely enough, mummies sometimes occur naturally. Normally, when a person dies, bacteria in the body start to multiply and the flesh decays or breaks down. If the bacteria can't get in, then there is no decay. Mummies have been found in ice, peat bogs, and sand—all places that prevent the bacteria needed to break down tissue. Some believe that seeing people and animals accidentally mummified in the hot desert sands might have inspired the ancient Egyptians to make mummies in the first place. What we do know is that the process and ritual of mummification evolved slowly throughout ancient Egyptian history.

Shabti

In addition to mummies, many small, mummy-like figurines were found inside tombs. These figures, made of wood, stone, wax, or faience, are called *shabti* and were typically about 6 to 10 inches long. Because the ancient Egyptians believed the dead needed the same things in the afterlife that they needed in real life, they buried *shabti* to do any necessary work for the dead person, such as harvesting food. When *shabti* first began to be used, in the Middle Kingdom, only one or two *shabti* would be placed in a tomb. By the New Kingdom, though, numerous *shabti* were placed in tombs. In some cases, there would be one for each day of the year! To hold all these figures, ancient Egyptians made special containers. Today, we call these containers *shabti* boxes.

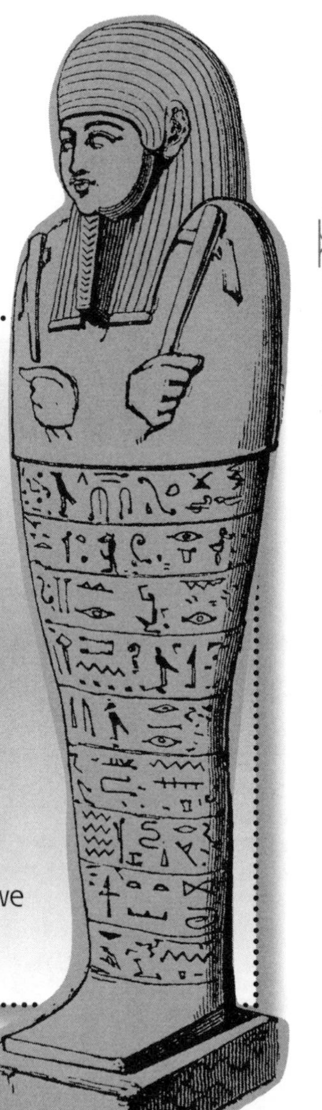

Did You Know?

Ancient Egyptians didn't just use natron for making mummies. They also used it to clean their bodies, teeth, and clothes, as well as to make glass and faience.

For example, the first mummies were merely wrapped, which did little, if anything, to prevent bacteria, and so the bodies still decayed under the bandages. During the Old Kingdom, the ancient Egyptians figured out how to use **natron** to preserve bodies. Natron was a natural kind of salt found deposited in and around ancient lakes, and it was the key ingredient in the ancient Egyptian mummification process.

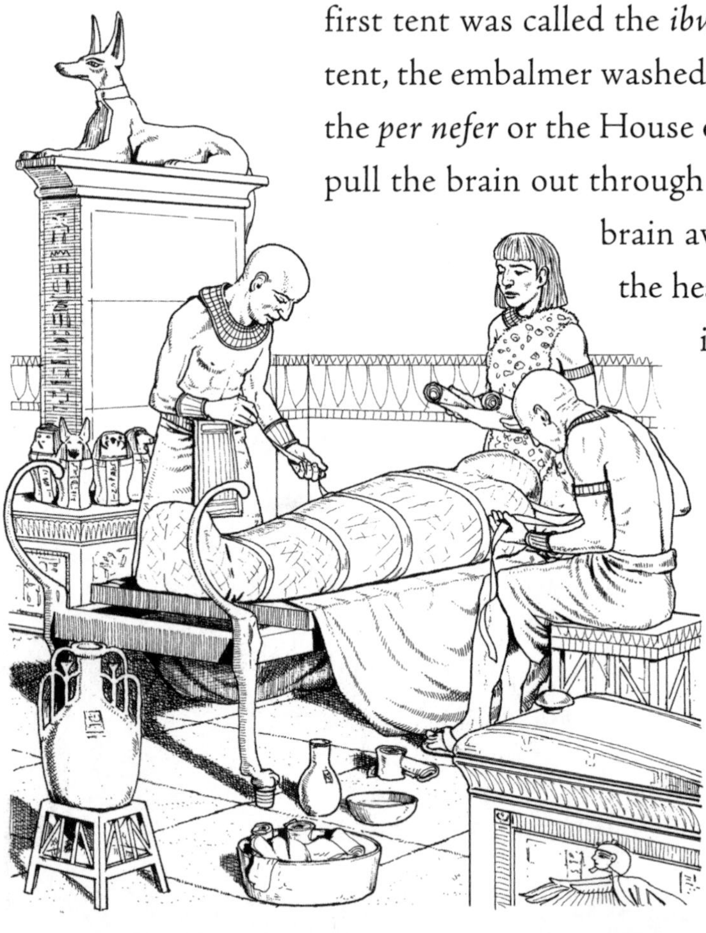

So, just what was this process? How were mummies made in ancient Egypt? When a person died, his or her body was taken to an **embalmer**. The embalmer brought the body to a group of tents that were set up way out in the desert. Being far away was important because the mummification process took 70 days and, not surprisingly, gave off a pretty unpleasant smell. The first tent was called the *ibw* or the Place of Purification. In this tent, the embalmer washed the body. The second tent was called the *per nefer* or the House of Beauty. Here, the embalmer would pull the brain out through the nose with a hook and throw the brain away. Then the other organs, except for the heart, were removed through a slit made in the side of the body. The heart, in which ancient Egyptians believed thought and feelings occurred, was vital to the deceased in the afterlife. The embalmer then placed the organs into **canopic jars**. These special jars were usually made of stone or clay. Each jar was decorated with a replica of one the "heads" of the four figures known as the sons of Horus. It was the job of the sons of Horus to guard the organs. Duamutef (the jackal-headed figure) protected the stomach, Qebehsenuef (the falcon-headed figure) protected the intestines, Hapy (the figure with the ape-like head) protected the lungs, and Imsety (the human-headed figure) protected the liver.

Canopic jars.

Once the organs were removed, the body was covered in and stuffed with natron, which dried out the body. After 40 days the natron was removed, and the body was stuffed with linen, straw, or sawdust. Pleasant-smelling spices or perfumes were added to the stuffing and the skin was rubbed with oils. Next, the skin was covered in melted resin, which is a natural, plastic-like substance from plants.

Finally, the bandaging could take place. The bandages used to wrap mummies were strips of linen several inches wide. The material was usually taken from old clothes, but if a family could afford it, new linen was used. Often, a combination of old and new linen was used, with the newer, nicer material reserved for the outermost layers. Each toe and finger was wrapped individually. Next, the arms and legs were wrapped. The arms were crossed over the chest and a copy of the Book of the Dead was sometimes placed between the legs. At last, the entire body was wrapped. Amulets were placed throughout

Words to Know

Ba: one of the elements that ancient Egyptians believed made up each person. The Ba is what we might call a person's personality.

Ka: the spiritual twin of the Ba that followed a person around unseen throughout his or her life.

Akh: formed when the Ba and Ka reunited after death.

Shadow: one of the elements that the ancient Egyptians believed made up each person. It was the Shadow's job to protect all the other elements or parts.

natron: a kind of salt that was the key ingredient in the mummification process.

embalmer: a person skilled in mummification.

canopic jars: special jars where the liver, lungs, stomach, and intestines of a dead person were kept after the organs were removed during mummification.

The Legend of Osiris

Osiris, the god of the underworld, sat on a throne and judged the deceased as they entered the afterlife. He was one of the most important gods of ancient Egypt. There are many versions of the story of how he came to be. But here is the most popular:

Osiris was once a real king who ruled Egypt. He ruled so well that his evil brother, Seth, was jealous. At a party, Seth tricked Osiris into climbing into a beautiful coffin by saying whoever could fit into it could have it. When Osiris got inside, Seth closed the box, sealed it, and threw it into the Nile. The box floated away, but Isis, Osiris's wife, found the coffin and brought it back to Egypt. When Seth discovered this, he was mad. He chopped Osiris's body into lots of parts and scattered them all over Egypt. Grief stricken, Isis searched and searched until she found most of the parts. Then, with help from some gods, Isis wrapped Osiris into a mummy, and he was magically brought back to life and sent to serve as ruler of the afterlife.

Horus, the son of Osiris and Isis, also had trouble with Seth. It is said that Seth tore out Horus's left eye during a fight. Thoth, another god, mended the eye. Horus eventually beat Seth. As a result, the eye, and Horus, became a symbol of protection. Known as the "eye of Horus," the "sacred eye," or the "udjat eye" it was a popular amulet. Even today, it continues to be a popular symbol. of protection and power.

Osiris, Seth, and Isis.

the multiple layers of linen. A scarab amulet was often placed over the heart because the scarab was the symbol of rebirth. The heart scarab was also important because it was engraved with a spell that prevented the mummy's heart from revealing its misdeeds to Osiris in the underworld.

When the mummy was completely wrapped, a funeral mask was

The eye of Horus.

placed over the head and shoulders. These masks were typically made or covered in gold and precious jewels and made to look like the deceased. King Tut's mask is probably one of the most famous funeral masks in history. Next, the mummy was covered in a shroud (a piece of cloth) and placed into a coffin, which was decorated with hieroglyphs and pictures, including a painting of the face of the deceased. Sometimes, the coffins were then placed into another coffin and everything placed inside a huge, stone box called a sarcophagus.

The heart scarab.

Once a body had been mummified, it was time for the funeral and burial. Like the mummification process, Egyptian funerals followed a very strict plan. On the appointed day, the family of the deceased followed behind the coffin as it was pulled on a sledge to the tomb. They cried loudly and tore their clothes to show their grief. Sometimes professional mourners were hired to wail! Behind the family were servants who carried offerings, such as food and furniture. Behind them came the canopic jars, which held the deceased's organs. Special dancers called *muu* dancers also danced along with the procession.

Once the mourners reached the burial spot, the coffin was stood upright and the Opening of the Mouth ceremony took place. This was a very important ritual; it allowed the deceased to use his or her mouth to speak and eat in the afterlife. During the Opening of the Mouth, a priest would touch a special stone tool called a *pesesh-kef* to the mummy's mouth or to a picture of the person's mouth on the outside of the coffin. The mouth was not

Ancient Egyptian women mourning for the dead.

actually opened. Next, the mummy was placed upright in the tomb. The tomb was sealed, and the mourners had a feast to celebrate the deceased being reborn in the afterlife.

For the deceased, getting to the tomb was only half the battle. The ancient Egyptians believed that, in the afterlife, they met Osiris, god of the underworld, in the Hall of Two

If King Tut's Mummy Could Talk

Mummies can't talk, of course, but they *can* tell us all kinds of things about ancient Egypt. Using modern-day techniques and equipment, archaeologists can learn about the kinds of illness and disease that existed thousands of years ago and determine the life expectancy of ancient Egyptians. Sometimes, mummies can even tell us how the person died.

One of the most famous mummies in the world is that of King Tut. Because he died at a young age, *how* he died has been a mystery hotly debated. For many years, people suspected the boy king might have been murdered. One of the things that made this theory believable was the fact that King Tut's skull showed damage, as if he might have been hit in the back of the head. In 2005, archaeologists used a CAT scan to examine his mummy. A CAT scan is a machine that takes lots of X-rays and then uses a computer to make those images into a three-dimensional picture. What did they find? They discovered that King Tut's body showed no sign of foul play. The king did have a broken leg, and it's possible the injury caused an infection, which then killed him. It's also possible that King Tut was poisoned, and experts are planning to test this theory by examining King Tut's organs.

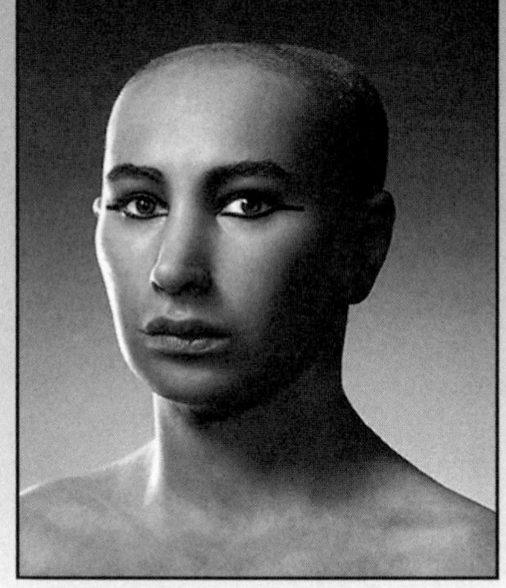

A reconstruction of Tut's face based on information provided by CAT scan.

But what about the damage to the back of King Tut's skull? Experts now believe that Howard Carter and his

Truths. As Osiris sat on a throne, 42 judges quizzed you about your life and whether you had been good and worthy. Next, Anubis, a jackal-headed god, placed your heart on one side of a scale. On the other side of the scale was Ma'at's feather of truth. (Ma'at was the goddess of truth, justice, and order.) The ancient Egyptians believed that if the

Did You Know?

Animals were mummified so they could join their owners in the afterlife. Mummies of dogs, cats, birds, crocodiles, and bulls have been discovered. The mummy of a scarab beetle has even been found!

team damaged the skull when they discovered King Tut's tomb and pulled the mummy out of the coffin. Because the mummy was stuck to the coffin with resin, it was yanked out too roughly.

Along with a treasure, King Tut's tomb was said to come with something else—a curse. Although it has never been proven, there was supposedly a curse written on a tablet on the outside of the tomb: "Death shall come on swift wings to him who disturbs the peace of the king." The idea that King Tut was getting his revenge on those who opened his tomb was fueled, in large part, by the death of Lord Carnarvon—one of the men who helped find King Tut's tomb—just months after the tomb was opened. He was bitten by a mosquito, got an infection, and died less than 6 months after the tomb was opened. Even though Lord Carnarvon had been in poor health long before the tomb was opened, people decided his death was proof of the curse. Soon, more rumors were flying. Two of the most famous ones are that at the moment Carnarvon died, the lights went out all over Cairo, and that Howard Carter's pet bird was eaten by a cobra, a symbol of the pharaohs. But these are just rumors.

Other folks connected to the opening of the tomb also fell ill, but no one else suffered an untimely death. In recent years, scientists have suggested that a bacteria or mold sickened tomb visitors. It is interesting to note that Howard Carter, the man who actually opened the tomb, lived another 17 years following the famous discovery.

Howard Carter and Lord Carnarvon.

Anubis weighing the heart of a dead person against Ma'at's Feather of Truth.

Did You Know?

Even people who came from other lands to live in Egypt embraced mummification. Distinctive paintings were put on the coffins of Greek and Roman settlers of ancient Egypt. These realistic portraits are called Fayum portraits and let us see what the mummified person looked like in life.

heart was lighter than the feather, the person got to move on to heaven. If the heart was heavier than the feather then a terrible beast ate the deceased!

Mummification was expensive, and only the wealthy could afford it. The poor were buried in simple coffins or in the sand. Still, there were many mummies made in ancient Egypt. Today, however, many of those mummies have disappeared, and there are several reasons for that. One reason is that mummies have been popular souvenir items. People bought them for their private collections, and many were lost or damaged. Another reason is that in the twelfth century, mummies were prized as an ingredient in medicines and were often ground up for this purpose.

Ma'at, the goddess of truth and justice.

Make Your Own *Shabti*

1 Unwrap the soap and grate the entire bar onto a sheet of wax paper. Be careful not to put your fingers too close to the food grater's edges.

2 After the bar is shredded, put your hands into the warm water. Let them get drippy wet. Pick up a handful of soap flakes, and squeeze them tightly. Add some water with your hands. Keep squeezing and adding water until you can begin to mold the soap. You'll need a fair amount of water to get the flakes to a modeling consistency, but DON'T pour water directly into the soap flakes. Use your hands to add water little by little.

3 Once your soap flakes are holding together you can start to mold a *shabti*. Remember, *shabti* looked like mummies, so you don't need to give them distinct arms and legs. In general, mummies are a little wider on the top than the bottom. Don't worry about facial details as you'll do these later.

4 If you want to have your *shabti* stand up, gently rub the bottom to make flat "feet." You can also make feet by rubbing the *shabti* on wax paper, but just be careful, because the soap figure will fall apart easily at this point.

5 When you are happy with your *shabti*, wet your hands one more time and gently rub it smooth before putting it on another sheet of wax paper to harden.

6 When the soap figure is nearly hardened, use a toothpick to carve details like a face, crossed arms, or hieroglyphs.

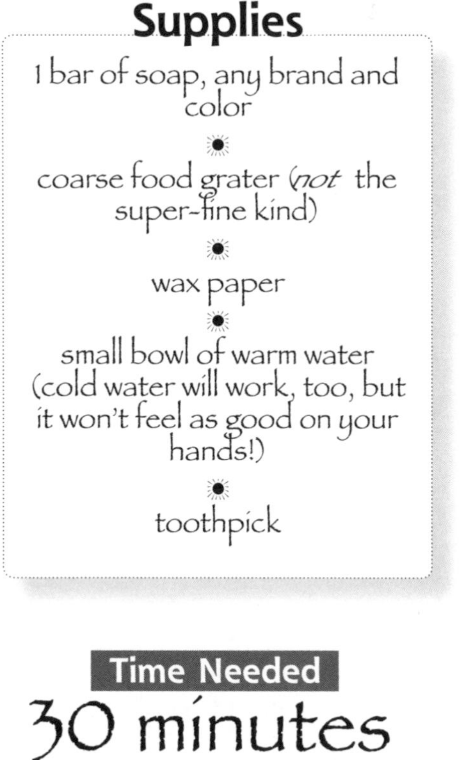

Supplies

1 bar of soap, any brand and color

coarse food grater (*not* the super-fine kind)

wax paper

small bowl of warm water (cold water will work, too, but it won't feel as good on your hands!)

toothpick

Did You Know?

The word mummy comes from the Arab word *mummiya*, which refers to bitumen or tar. The resin the ancient Egyptians used on mummies gave them a tar-like appearance.

Time Needed

30 minutes

Make Your Own

Funeral Mask

1 After covering your workspace with plenty of newspaper, cut off the bottom of your milk jug so you have about a 2-inch "bowl." Turn the bowl over onto the newspaper. This will be part of the base for your mask.

2 Roll up the kitchen towel, lengthwise. If you don't have a towel, you can also use rolled up newspaper or plastic grocery bags. Wrap it around the milk jug bottom. This will serve as the base for the *nemes* around your funeral mask. (Remember, a *nemes* is the royal headwear of pharaohs.)

3 Use several sheets of foil to completely cover the milk jug and towel. Tuck and scrunch the foil to form the face for your funeral mask. Don't forget to include a nose and a false beard. Don't worry about attaching the features; you only need them to help mold the plaster cloth.

4 When you're happy with the face, cut the plaster cloth into triangles. (Triangular pieces will lay flat over just about any surface of your mask, while rectangular pieces sometimes bunch.) Dip the pieces of cloth into the water and apply to the mask according to the directions on the package. Smooth any bumps with wet fingers, and then allow the mask to dry completely.

5 Carefully remove the mask from the foil. Use more strips of plaster cloth for any needed repairs. After the mask has hardened, trim off any extra cloth.

6 Decorate your mask any way you'd like. Add kohl eyes and other facial details. If you want, you can add imitation jewels to your funeral mask as well. (Note: permanent markers work best on spray-painted surfaces.)

Supplies

- newspaper
- plastic 1-gallon milk jug, rinsed and dried
- scissors
- kitchen towel
- aluminum foil
- 1 large roll of plaster cloth, sometimes called plaster gauze (you can find this with the plaster of Paris in many craft, hobby, or art supply stores—Rigid Wrap is one brand name)
- shallow bowl of water
- decorating materials, such as gold spray paint, markers, acrylic paint, and plastic beads

Time Needed

45 minutes

not including drying and painting time

16 Hieroglyphs

Along with pyramids and mummies, the ancient Egyptians are remembered for their written language: a beautiful and mysterious-looking script that covered the walls of tombs, temples, and coffins. The pictures and symbols that made up ancient Egypt's earliest form of writing are called hieroglyphs. (The word hieroglyph translates to mean "sacred carving.") There are hundreds of hieroglyphs, divided into three categories called phonograms, logograms, and determinatives.

Phonograms are symbols that represent a sound. Like our alphabet, there are a few dozen symbols that each represent one sound. For example, a picture of an owl represented the "m" sound. Most of the other symbols represent a combination of either two or three consonant sounds.

Logograms are also known as ideagrams, and are symbols that represent the word they look like. For example, the symbol for a house looks kind of like a flat-roofed house. Logograms

man

woman

god, king

force, effort

eat, drink, speak

Some determinative symbols.

Did You Know?

Ancient Egyptian writing followed grammar rules that are very different from those in English. It would be a challenging language for most people to learn today.

don't tell us how to pronounce a word.

Determinatives help define or clarify a word. For example, the ancient Egyptians might write a name and then follow it with the symbol of a man so readers knew the person was a man.

Hieroglyphs were mainly used in formal writing, such as on tomb walls. They were written in horizontal rows and vertical columns without punctuation! They could be written from right to left or left to right. To indicate which direction a reader should read, a writer drew the faces of animals and people toward the beginning of the sentence. For example, if the faces were facing to the left, a reader knew to read from left to right.

As ancient Egyptian culture evolved, so did their language and writing. A shorthand version of hieroglyphs called **hieratic script** came into use. Unlike hieroglyphs, it was always read from right to left. More cursive in style, hieratic script made it easier to write quickly, especially on papyrus and ostraca. Hieratic script was used for everyday documents like letters and for business or government records. Next, around 700 BCE, came **demotic script**. Because it used more phonetic symbols that represented sounds in spoken language, more people could read demotic script. *Demotic* means "common or popular." Later on, around the time Egypt was ruled by the Ptolemies (305–30 BCE), Coptic script was invented by combining the Greek alphabet and demotic script.

Ⲁⲁ	Ⲃⲃ	Ⲅⲅ	Ⲇⲇ	Ⲉⲉ	ⲋ	Ⲍⲍ	Ⲏⲏ	Ⲑⲑ	Ⲓⲓ	Ⲕⲕ
a	b, v	g, gh, ng	th, d	e	6	z	ee	th, t	i, y	k
Ⲗⲗ	Ⲙⲙ	Ⲛⲛ	Ⲝⲝ	Ⲟⲟ	Ⲡⲡ	Ⲣⲣ	Ⲥⲥ	Ⲧⲧ	Ⲩⲩ	Ⲫⲫ
l	m	n	x	o (short)	p	r	s	t, d	v, u, y	f
Ⲭⲭ	Ⲯⲯ	Ⲱⲱ	Ϣϣ	Ϥϥ	Ϧϧ	Ϩϩ	Ϭϭ	Ϯϯ	Ϫϫ	`
k, sh, kh	ps	o (long)	sh	f	kh	h	ch	tee	g, j	

Coptic script.

Very few ancient Egyptians could read and write. (Some estimate the number to be one out of a hundred people.) That job was left to scribes, and for that reason the

Did You Know?

Scribes are often shown in pictures and as statues in a seated position with a piece of papyrus rolled across their laps.

scribes were incredibly important! They were in charge of things like copying texts, writing important letters, paying workers and keeping track of accounts, collecting taxes, recording the outcomes of court cases, and organizing the building of pyramids and temples. Scribes were highly respected. It has been suggested, though, that scribes guarded their knowledge of reading and writing tightly, and kept it to themselves in order to maintain a position of power in the community. After all, if more people could read and write, scribes wouldn't be needed as much.

Scribe with an inkstand.

Scribes typically came from wealthy or powerful families, and the position was often passed from father to son. Boys began their training to become scribes at a young age, around 10 years old. They attended training at another scribe's house or at a temple. (Being a scribe was the only job in ancient Egypt that people went to school for. All other professions were learned through an apprenticeship.) Boys learned to read and write by memorizing texts and copying scripts. Because papyrus was too expensive to practice on, boys wrote on less valuable ostraca.

A scribe's palette was a narrow, rectangular piece of wood or stone that had two shallow wells

Words to Know

phonogram: the type of hieroglyph that represents a sound.

logogram: the type of hieroglyph that represents the word it looks like.

determinative: the type of hieroglyph that helps define or clarify a word.

hieratic script: a shorthand, cursive style of hieroglyphic script. It was used for everyday documents like letters and business or government records.

demotic script: a cursive form of ancient Egyptian writing and one of the three scripts found on the Rosetta stone.

for ink. Black ink was often made with soot, and red ink was made from red ochre. Water was mixed with these solids to make ink. There was a slit down the middle of the palette to hold the pens, which were brushes made with pounded or chewed reeds. It could take as many as 10 years to learn all the hieroglyphic signs and the other subjects scribes needed to know, such as mathematics, astrology, astronomy, and art. Teachers were strict and often used physical punishment on students who did poorly at a lesson.

Words to Know

Rosetta stone: a stone found in 1799 that had the same decree written in three different languages: hieroglyphs, demotic script, and Greek. It was the key to unlocking the mysteries of ancient Egypt's written language.

After the Romans took over Egypt in 30 BCE, Egypt was gradually converted to Christianity, and Egyptian writing was eventually banned. Since no one was reading and writing it, hieroglyphs were forgotten. The meaning of the many hieroglyphs of ancient Egypt might have been lost forever if it hadn't been for the **Rosetta stone** and the French scholar named Jean-François Champollion who translated it.

Jean-François Champollion

The Rosetta stone is a large carved stone that was found in 1799 in the western delta of Egypt near the town of Rosetta. It is a piece of a larger stone and is about 45 inches high, 28.5 inches wide, and 11 inches thick. (The larger stone from which it broke off has not been found.) Carved on the Rosetta stone is a decree celebrating the 1-year anniversary of the coronation of Ptolemy V. But what's so remarkable about the Rosetta stone is that the decree is written in three different languages: hieroglyphs, demotic script, and Greek.

Did You Know?

Because we don't know the sounds that certain hieroglyphic symbols represented, and because the language didn't use vowels, no one knows for certain what the spoken ancient Egyptian language *sounded* like! To make words easier to pronounce, Egyptologists added "e" or "a" to them.

The Rosetta stone.

Jean-François Champollion had a lifelong love of language, and by studying these three scripts, he was able to break the long-forgotten code of hieroglyphs in 1822. (As the story goes, he had wanted to decode hieroglyphs ever since he was a boy and saw them on a temple!) Once people could finally read what was written on the tombs and papyri, they were able to learn a tremendous amount about the culture of the ancient Egyptians. It's fair to say that Champollion was one of the pioneers of Egyptology. Today, you can see the Rosetta stone for yourself at the British Museum in London.

Numbers in Ancient Egypt

Much of what we know about the ancient Egyptian number system and mathematics comes from studying several papyri, including the Rhind papyrus. Like our mathematical system, the ancient Egyptian system worked in base 10. They used pictures or symbols to represent numbers. For numbers 1 through 9, they made strokes. (One stroke or line for 1, two strokes for 2, and so on.) The number 10 was represented by a hobble for cattle (the symbol looks like an upside down letter "u"). The sign for 100 was a coil of rope. A lotus plant represented 1,000. A frog or tadpole was the symbol for 100,000. And 1,000,000 was conveyed by a god with his arms raised above his head. Numbers were usually placed largest to smallest, but it didn't really matter. Ancient Egyptians used what was called a simple grouping or additive system; it didn't rely on positional values. And because their numbers didn't rely on positional value, they didn't need zero. For example, when we write 101, zero marks the tens' value. But in ancient Egypt, that number would be written as one coil of rope and one stroke.

As with their writing, ancient Egyptians eventually found they needed a faster, more efficient way to represent numbers. So they came up with hieratic numerals. In this system, there were symbols for 1–10, 20, 30, 40, 50, 60, 70, 80, 90, 100, 200, 300, 400, 500, 600, 700, 800, 900, 1000, 2000, 3000, 4000, 5000, 6000, 7000, 8000, and 9000.

Make Your Own Ostraca

1 Turn your plant saucer over and place it on a few sheets of newspaper. Remove any price stickers and clean away any dirt with a wet rag. Make sure the saucer dries completely before moving on to the next step.

2 Paint the dish according to the directions on the chalkboard paint can. (It will probably need several coats.)

3 Let the paint dry completely. Now you can practice writing hieroglyphs on its surface just like ancient Egyptian scribes did!

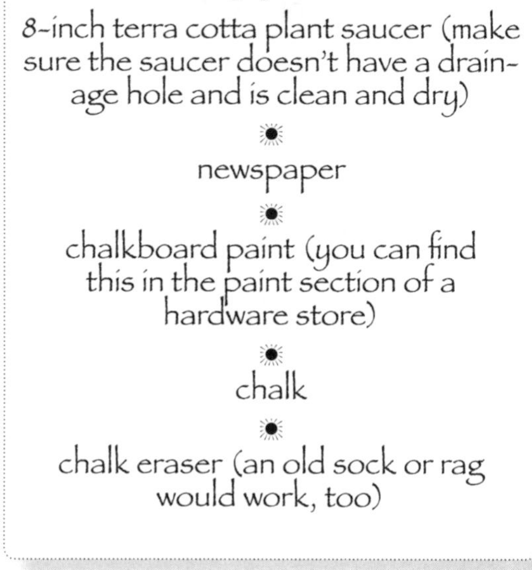

Supplies

8-inch terra cotta plant saucer (make sure the saucer doesn't have a drainage hole and is clean and dry)

newspaper

chalkboard paint (you can find this in the paint section of a hardware store)

chalk

chalk eraser (an old sock or rag would work, too)

Time Needed
10 minutes
not including drying time

Make Your Own Egyptian Mural

Because hieroglyphs were usually carved into the stone, it wasn't a good thing to make a mistake! Scribes and stonemasons had to be careful. To help make sure the work turned out the right way, they used grids to guide them. You can use the same technique to make an Egyptian wall mural.

1 Sketch out what you want on your mural onto the graph paper. (Don't make it too tiny!) Tomb walls often told stories about what would happen as the deceased traveled into the afterlife. Combine pictures and hieroglyphs.

2 When you're finished drawing, use the ruler and red pencil to make a grid of 1-inch squares. This grid goes right on top of your pictures and hieroglyphs.

3 Unroll the butcher paper until you have the desired size, and cut the piece from the roll. Tack or tape the paper up on a wall. Hang it so you can comfortably reach the top of the paper.

4 Use the chalk-line reel to make a grid of squares. You'll need the same number of squares on your butcher paper as on your graph paper. They shouldn't be the same size, though. For example, if you want to make your mural twice as big as your design, make the squares on the butcher paper 2 inches by 2 inches; if you want it to be four times bigger, make your squares 4 inches by 4 inches; and so on. Use the ruler to make marks along the top, bottom, and sides of the paper that are the desired length apart.

5 To make a chalk-line grid, you'll need someone to help you. Pull the string out of the reel and line it up against the paper, touching the top and bottom marks. Hold it tight at both ends, then pull the string out about 5 inches and let it go. It will snap back against the paper and leave a chalk line. Make horizontal lines the same way.

6 Using your graph paper as a guide, sketch your mural. You can do this by copying one section from your graph into the corresponding section of the chalk-line grid.

7 When you have the whole picture transferred, gently brush away the chalk lines. Now, you can paint or use markers to make your Egyptian mural colorful!

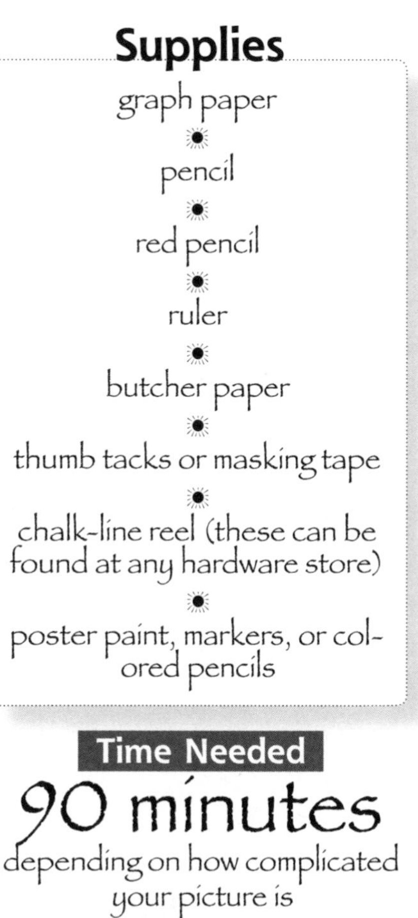

Supplies

graph paper

pencil

red pencil

ruler

butcher paper

thumb tacks or masking tape

chalk-line reel (these can be found at any hardware store)

poster paint, markers, or colored pencils

Time Needed

90 minutes

depending on how complicated your picture is

Make Your Own Cartouche

A cartouche for Rameses the Great.

A cartouche is the oval-shaped symbol that surrounds the names of kings in hieroglyphs. Some tombs in the Valley of the Kings are even cartouche shaped. In this project, you can carve your own name into "stone."

1 Curve your cardboard to make a skinny "O" shape. Overlap the ends and use a piece of tape to secure them together. It's okay if it's not exactly an oval; you can smooth the edges later on. Lay the cardboard oval on a piece of wax paper. This will be your mold.

2 Mix two parts plaster of Paris to one part water. If you are using a 12-inch-long piece of cardboard, you'll need ½ cup plaster of Paris mix and ¼ cup water. Mix well. Hold the cardboard mold flat against the wax paper and pour the plaster inside. Fill about half way. Hold the mold securely against the wax paper for a few minutes, or until the plaster just begins to set.

3 Allow the plaster to cure in the mold for about 45 minutes to an hour. Check it frequently to make sure it's not getting too dry. When the top has just lost its glossy, wet look, it's time to peel away the wax paper and carve it on that side. Use a pushpin or long needle to carve hieroglyphic symbols to make your name. (A toothpick will work in a pinch, but it will be harder to carve details.) Remember, the ancient Egyptians didn't use vowels, but you can if you'd like. As you work, clean the tip of your pushpin frequently and gently brush or blow away the bits of plaster that have been carved out.

4 After you've carved your name, carefully pull off the masking tape and cardboard. The plaster should hold its shape at this point. If it doesn't, leave the cardboard mold on for another 15 minutes.

5 Let your cartouche air dry. When it's done, you can use sandpaper to gently round any sharp edges. Add color by following the grooves of the hieroglyphs with markers or paint. You can decorate the edges of the cartouche, too.

Go to www.upennmuseum/hieroglyphsreal.cgi to translate into hieroglyphs.

Supplies

- piece of thick cardboard, 1 inch wide and about 12 inches long (or longer if you have a long name)
- masking tape
- wax paper
- plaster of Paris
- water
- mixing bowl and spoon (or bucket and paint stirrer)
- pushpin or needle
- sandpaper, markers, and paint

Time Needed

25 minutes

not including drying time

Glossary

A

absolute power: complete control over a government and/or organized group of people.
Akh: one of the elements the ancient Egyptians believed made up each person. The Akh was what was formed when the Ba and Ka reunited after death.
***Akhet*:** what the ancient Egyptians called the flooding season, from June to September.
ankh: the hieroglyphic symbol that means "life" and also refers to the amulet made in the shape of the hieroglyph.
Akhenaton: a king who ruled from 1352 to 1336 BCE. He was known as the "Heretic King" because during his rule he called for the worship of just one god instead of many. He was also the father of Tutankhamen.
amulet: special charms that have magic powers to protect, heal, or give the wearer a desired characteristic.
Amun: in Egyptian mythology, the supreme god and the god of the sun. Also known as Ra and Amun-Ra.
Anubis: the jackal-headed god who looked after the dead and oversaw mummification.
archaeologist: someone who studies ancient people and their cultures.
artifacts: hand-made objects that are still around from a particular time period.

B

BCE: the abbreviation for Before Common Era when the years count down to zero. BCE means the same things as BC, or "Before Christ."
Ba: one of the elements that ancient Egyptians believed made up each person. The Ba is what we might call a person's personality.
bark shrine: a special, boat-shaped carrier that housed the *naos* (or box) where the statue of a god was kept when it was carried through the streets on festival days.
bartering system: a system in which people trade goods for goods rather than goods for money.
Bastet: a cat goddess who had the body of a woman and the head of a cat.
Bes: the dwarf-like god of children and fun and games. Bes was a popular household god in ancient Egypt.
Book of the Dead: a collection of spells, formulas, magical texts, and illustrations written on papyrus, which the ancient Egyptians used as a guidebook to the afterlife and funeral rituals.
Book of Instruction: a collection of writings that provided advice for kids on how to succeed and live a moral life.

C

CE: abbreviation for Common Era when the years count up from zero. It means the same thing as AD ("anno Domini").
canopic jars: special jars where the liver, lungs, stomach, and intestines of a dead person were kept after the organs were removed during mummification.
cartouche: the oval-shaped symbol that surrounds the names of kings in hieroglyphs.
Cleopatra: a Greek queen who ruled Egypt from around 51 to 30 BCE. She was the last pharaoh.
Coptic script: a combination of the Greek alphabet and demotic script.
crook: (*heka scepter*) an item often carried by kings and considered a symbol for "rule" or "ruler." It looked like a short cane or shepherd's staff.

D

***deben*:** a weight usually made of copper that the ancient Egyptians used in their bartering system.
delta: a triangular-shaped area where a river fans out and divides as it flows into a larger body of water.
demotic: a cursive form of ancient Egyptian writing and one of the three scripts found on the Rosetta stone.
***deshret*:** what the ancient Egyptians called the desert. It translates to "Red Land." The crown worn by the king of Lower Egypt was also called *deshret*. *See* red crown.
determinative: the type of hieroglyph that helps define or clarify a word.

diadem: a type of headband worn by ancient Egyptians.
djed: an amulet with a vertical base and four lines at the top. Some believe it looks like a back (a spine) and was worn to protect that part of the body.
double crown: (*pschent*) the crown worn by ancient Egyptian kings after Upper and Lower Egypt were united. It is a combination of the white and red crowns.
dung beetle: a beetle considered the symbol of rebirth because it "magically" appeared from dung. The ancient Egyptians didn't know that dung beetles laid their eggs in dung.

E

Egyptologist: an archaeologist who specializes in Egyptology, or the study of ancient Egypt.
embalmer: a person skilled in mummification.
eye of Horus: (*udjat* or the Sacred Eye) a very popular ancient Egyptian amulet that resembled the eye that Horus lost in a fight and then had magically restored.

F

faience: a glazed, non-clay ceramic material the Egyptians used to make beads, jars, art, and amulets.
false door: a fake, recessed doorway in temples and pyramids where funeral offerings were made.
flail: (*nekhakha*) an item often carried by kings, along with their crook, as a symbol of power. It looked like a short rod with three beaded strands attached.
flax: a plant whose seed was used to make oil and whose fibers were made into linen cloth.

H

Hapy: the Egyptian god of the Nile and inundation.
Hatshepsut: the first known woman to be an ancient Egyptian pharaoh. She ruled from about 1473 to 1458 BCE.
henna: the tree or the dye made from the tree used by the ancient Egyptians to make cosmetics and skin and hair dye.
hieratic: a shorthand, cursive style of hieroglyphic script. It was used for everyday documents like letters and business or government records.
hieroglyphs: the pictures and symbols that made up ancient Egypt's earliest form of writing. Hieroglyph means "sacred writing," and often covered coffins and the walls of tombs and temples.
Horus: a falcon god and the son of Osiris, the head of the underworld.
Hounds and Jackals: an ancient Egyptian game similar to today's Chutes and Ladders.

I

incense: a mixture of wood, bark, spices, oil, and resin that was burned or left on hot coals to smolder and create a pleasant smell.
inundation: the annual flooding of the Nile during ancient times.
irrigate: to supply water by diverting streams or digging canals.
Isis: the ancient Egyptian goddess of motherhood. She was Osiris's wife and Horus's mother.

K

Ka: one of the elements that the ancient Egyptians believed made up a person. It is best described as a spiritual twin or shadow.
Kemet: what the ancient Egyptians called their land. It means "Black Land," and was named this because of the silt left behind during flooding.
khamsin: hot winds that raise the air temperature and cause terrible sandstorms during Egypt's spring.
Khufu: (also know as Cheops) an ancient Egyptian king who ruled from 2589 to 2566 BCE and built the Great Pyramid at Giza.
Kid is Made to Fall: an ancient Egyptian game in which children sat on the ground with their arms outstretched, trying to knock over a child who would be attempting to jump over them.
kilt: a wraparound-style skirt, worn by both men and women, that is either tied, pinned, tucked in, or held up with a sash.
King Tut: *see* Tutankhamen.
kohl: the dark powder the ancient Egyptians used to make thick, long lines around their eyes and out to

the sides of their faces. It was made from ground up galena, a silver-gray mineral.
kohl pot: the jars where kohl was kept. Several dating back from ancient Egypt have been discovered.
khuzza lawizza: a game like leapfrog played by ancient Egyptian children.

L

Late Period: a recognized time period in ancient Egypt from 644 to 332 BCE.
Library of Alexandria: several buildings that reportedly housed 500,000 books and were a place where great thinkers met. It was built by Ptolomy I Soter around 288 BCE and later destroyed by a series of fires.
linen: fabric woven with fibers from the flax plant.
logogram: the type of hieroglyph that represents the word it looks like.
Lower Egypt: the land near the Nile's delta, in the northern part of ancient Egypt.

M

Ma'at: the goddess and concept of truth, justice, and order.
Mancala: an ancient game that uses a game board with holes and small stones for counting.
mastaba: rectangular, aboveground, brick tombs.
Mehen: an ancient Egyptian game played on a one-legged table with a top that looked like a coiled snake. The snake's body was divided into squares, and players moved their pieces along these squares.
Middle Kingdom: the time period from 2055 to 1650 BCE in ancient Egypt.
mudbricks: bricks made of sun-dried mud and other materials, such as pebbles and straw.
mummification: the process of drying and preserving a body.

N

natron: a natural, powder-like compound found deposited in and near ancient lakes. It was a kind of salt and the key ingredient in the mummification process.
***nemes*:** a head covering that ancient Egyptian royalty wore.
New Kingdom: the time period from 1550 to 1069 BCE in ancient Egypt.
Nile River: the longest river in the world and the reason the ancient Egyptians survived and thrived so well.

O

obelisk: a tall, skinny, solid stone monument with a pointed top that resembles a pyramid. The ancient Egyptians often placed them next to temples or tombs.
Old Kingdom: the time period from 2686 to 2181 BCE in ancient Egypt.
Osiris: the god of the underworld and husband of Isis. Ancient Egyptians believed he sat on a throne and judged the deceased as they entered the afterlife.
ostraca: broken pottery or stones that the ancient Egyptians wrote on.

P

papyrus: a tall, marsh plant the ancient Egyptians used to make boats and paper. Also the actual paper made from the plant.
Peret: what the ancient Egyptians called their growing season, from October to February. It was also called the Season of Emergence.
pharaoh: the ancient Egyptian name for king.
Pharos: another name for the Lighthouse of Alexandria, one of the Seven Wonders of the Ancient World. The name eventually came to mean lighthouse in many languages.
phonogram: the type of hieroglyph that represents a sound.
primeval mound: a sacred and mythical mound where the ancient Egyptians believed the sun first rose and life was created.
pyramids: monuments that house the tomb of ancient Egyptian pharaohs, as well as all the things he or she needed in the afterlife. There were three types of pyramids built in ancient Egypt: step pyramids, bent pyramids, and true pyramids.
pyramid text: sacred writing on the inner walls of pyramids.

R

Ra: (sometimes spelled *Re* or *Rah*) the ancient Egyptian sun god.
Rameses II: (Rameses the Great) a pharaoh who ruled from 1279 to 1213 BCE. He was responsible for more monuments and temples than any other king.
red crown: (*deshret*) the crown worn by the king of Lower Egypt.
Rosetta stone: a stone found in 1799 that had the same decree written in three different languages:

hieroglyphs, demotic script, and Greek. Translated by Jean-François Champollion, it was the key to unlocking the mysteries of ancient Egypt's written language.

S

sarcophagus: a large stone box where coffins were placed.
scarab: a very popular ancient Egyptian amulet that honored the dung beetle and life and rebirth.
scribes: ancient Egyptians who read and wrote hieroglyphs.
scroll: pieces of papyrus glued together and then rolled up. These were the first books.
Sekhmet: a cat goddess who had the body of a woman and the head of a lion. She was the goddess of war or battle.
Senet: a board game that was popular in ancient Egypt and is still enjoyed today by people all over the world.
***shabti*:** small, mummy-like figures found inside tombs. It was the *shabti's* responsibility to do any necessary work of the deceased. They were also called *ushabti* or *shawabti*.
Shadow: one of the elements that the ancient Egyptians believed made up each person. It was the Shadow's job to protect all the other elements or parts.
shaduf: an irrigation device that the ancient Egyptians used to water their crops.
sheath dress: a common ancient Egyptian dress worn by women.
***Shemu*:** what the ancient Egyptians called their harvesting season, from March to May.
side-lock of youth: the S-shaped curl that children in ancient Egypt wore on the side of their heads.
Sirius: a star whose annual appearance in the sky was relied upon for the ancient Egyptian calendar.
sledge: a simple machine that uses logs and a platform to move heavy objects.
sphinx: an ancient Egyptian image in the form of a lion having a man's head, or a ram's or hawk's head.

T

Taweret: the ancient Egyptian goddess of women, children, and fertility. She had the head and body of a pregnant hippo, paws like a lion, and the back of crocodile.
temples: buildings that ancient Egyptians made so that gods had a place to live. Temples were more than a place where people could leave offerings—they were also gathering places in the community.
trachoma: a disease that causes blindness and has always been a problem in Egypt and other parts of the world due to poor diet and sanitation.
tunic: a piece of clothing worn by both men and women in ancient Egypt. Tunics looked like long T-shirts.
Tutankhamen (known as King Tut): a king who ruled from 1336 to 1327 BCE. His tomb is famous because it was found much later than most and was the only one *not* robbed in modern times.

U

udjat: also called the "eye of Horus," this was an amulet worn for health and overall protection. According to myth, it represents the eye of the god Horus that was torn out in a fight with his evil uncle and then magically restored.
underworld: the world of the dead.
Upper Egypt: the land in the Nile River Valley, in the southern part of ancient Egypt.
uraeus: the cobra featured on the double crown that represents the eye of Ra, the sun god.

V

Valley of the Kings: the remote area west of Thebes where people in the New Kingdom buried their kings with the hope that robbers would not find the tombs.
vizier: the ancient Egyptian's highest government office next to the king.

W

white crown: (*hedjet*) the crown that the king of Upper Egypt wore.
winnow: to separate grain from its husks by tossing it in the air or blowing air through it.
***wesekh*:** a wide, beaded collar and one of the most popular items of jewelry in ancient Egypt.

Resources

Books and Periodicals

Cole, Joanna. *The Magic School Bus, Ms. Frizzle's Adventures: Ancient Egypt*. New York: Scholastic Press Inc., 2001.

Collier, Mark & Manley, Bill. *How to Read Egyptian Hieroglyphs*. California: University of California Press, 1998.

Hagen, Rose-Marie and Rainer. *Egypt: People-Gods-Pharaohs*. California: Taschen America, 2005.

Hart, Avery & Mantell, Paul. *Pyramids! 50 Hands-On Activities to Experience Ancient Egypt*. Vermont: Williamson Publishing, 1997.

Hart, George (consulting editor). *Discoveries: Ancient Egypt*. California: Fog City Press, 2003.

Meltzer, Milton. *In the Days of the Pharaohs: A Look at Ancient Egypt*. New York: Franklin Watts, 2001.

Mertz, Barbara. *Red Land, Black Land: Daily Life in Ancient Egypt*. New York: Dodd, Mead & Company, revised 1978.

Mertz, Barbara. *Temples, Tombs and Hieroglyphs: A Popular History of Ancient Egypt*. New York: Dodd, Mead & Company, revised 1978.

Pemberton, Delia. *The Atlas of Ancient Egypt*. New York: Harry N. Abrams, Inc., 2005.

Ryan, Donald P. *The Complete Idiot's Guide to Ancient Egypt*. Indiana: Alpha Books, 2002.

Shaw, Ian & Nicholson, Paul. *The Dictionary of Ancient Egypt*. New York: Harry N. Abrams Inc., updated 2003.

The Egyptian Book of the Dead: The Book of Going Forth by Day. Images by Wasserman, James. Translated by Faulkner, Raymond and Goelet Jr., Ogden. Introduction by Andrews, Carol. California: Chronicle Books, revised 1998.

Williams, A.R., "Modern Technology Reopens the Ancient Case of King Tut." *National Geographic*, June 2005.

Web Sites

World's oldest boats—http://www.abc.se/~pa/mar/abydos.htm

Ancient Egyptian Boats—http://www.kingtutshop.com/freeinfo/egyptian-boats.htm

Ancient Egyptian Hairstyles—http://www.mnsu.edu/emuseum/prehistory/egypt/dailylife/hairstyles.html

Animal Mummies—http://www.animalmummies.com/

Aspects of Life in Ancient Egypt—http://nefertiti.iwebland.com/timelines/topics/index.html

British Museum—Ancient Egypt—http://www.ancientegypt.co.uk/

(The) Charm of the Amulet—http://www.touregypt.net/featurestories/amulets.htm

Egyptian Numerals—http://www-groups.dcs.st-and.ac.uk/~history/HistTopics/Egyptiannumerals.html

(The) Game of Senet—http://www.gamecabinet.com/history/Senet.html

(The) Great Lighthouse of Alexandria—http://www.unmuseum.org/pharos.htm

History for Kids—Ancient Egypt—http://www.historyforkids.org/learn/egypt/index.htm

Papyrus History—http://www.geocities.com/Hollywood/Location/8761/papyrushistory.html

Pyramids—the Inside Story—http://www.pbs.org/wgbh/nova/pyramid/

Return of Papyrus—http://www.saudiaramcoworld.com/issue/197304/the.return.of.papyrus.htm

Welcome to the Ancient Egyptian Home—http://egyptmonth.com/mag10012000/magf1.htm

Index

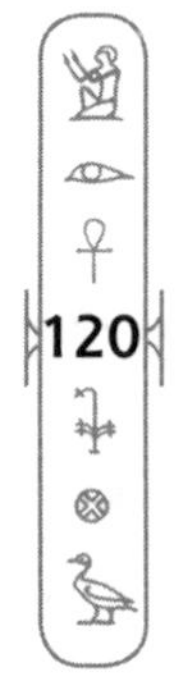